£7.99

π
-p+p

49

COLLECTED POEMS: 1

Peter Reading: Collected Poems

1: POEMS 1970-1984 (Bloodaxe Books, 1995):

Water and Waste (1970)
For the Municipality's Elderly (1974)
The Prison Cell & Barrel Mystery (1976)
Nothing For Anyone (1977)
Fiction (1979)
Tom o' Bedlam's Beauties (1981)
Diplopic (1983)
5x5x5x5x5 (1983)
C (1984)

2: POEMS 1985-1996 (Bloodaxe Books, 1996)

Ukulele Music (1985)
Going On (1985)
Stet (1986)
Final Demands (1988)
Perduta Gente (1989)
Shitheads (1989)
Evagatory (1992)
Last Poems (1994)
and new poems

—PETER READING—
Collected Poems
1: POEMS 1970-1984

BLOODAXE BOOKS

ISBN: 1 85224 320 1 hardback edition
       1 85224 321 X paperback edition

First published 1995 by
Bloodaxe Books Ltd,
P.O. Box 1SN,
Newcastle upon Tyne NE99 1SN.

Bloodaxe Books Ltd acknowledges
the financial assistance of Northern Arts.

Cover printing by J. Thomson Colour Printers Ltd, Glasgow.

Printed in Great Britain by
Cromwell Press Ltd, Broughton Gifford, Melksham, Wiltshire.

To Angela Reading

ACKNOWLEDGEMENTS

The books which comprise volume 1 of Peter Reading's *Collected Poems* were first published as individual collections by the following publishers:

OUTPOSTS PUBLICATIONS:
Water and Waste (1970)

MARTIN SECKER & WARBURG LTD:
For the Municipality's Elderly (1974)
The Prison Cell & Barrel Mystery (1976)
Nothing For Anyone (1977)
Fiction (1979)
Tom o' Bedlam's Beauties (1981)
Diplopic (1983)
C (1984)

CEOLFRITH PRESS:
5x5x5x5x5 (1983) with images by David Butler

Some poems from the first eight collections were later republished in *Essential Reading* (Secker & Warburg, 1986). *Diplopic* and *C* were reprinted, with *Ukulele Music* (1985), as parts of *3 in 1* (Chatto & Windus, 1992). Three poems from *Water and Waste*, 'Horticulture', 'Dead Horse' and 'Dirty Linen', are collected here as part of *For the Municipality's Elderly,* but were not published in that collection. 'Chiaroscuro' in *For the Municipality's Elderly* was first published in *Water and Waste* as 'Photogravure'.

CONTENTS

THE PRISON CELL & BARREL MYSTERY (1976)

NOTHING FOR ANYONE (1977)

DIPLOPIC (1983)

5x5x5x5x5 (1983)

C (1984)

Index of titles and first lines
See Collected Poems: 2

INTRODUCTION

These *Collected Poems* celebrate Peter Reading's 50th birthday and 25 years of outstanding poetic achievement by one of Britain's most prolific, versatile, startlingly contemporary and strikingly original poets.

It is doubly commendable that his 17 volumes of poetry published from 1970 to 1994 should appear together because the most distinguishing hallmark of Reading's art is its absolute unity. Each of his books is unified by one major theme, careful antithetical or polyphonic plotting, and highly sophisticated structures. Cohesion is achieved by the continual cross-referencing of narrative, imagery, motifs, voices and verbal echoes, an interweaving more commonly found in novels. This cross-referencing becomes even more ambitious in the later books, where it is part of the presentation: starting with *Final Demands*, Reading's first publisher Secker & Warburg (to be followed by Chatto & Windus as from *Evagatory*) was ready to accept bromides that Reading had prepared himself. This enabled him to produce different kinds of layout and typesetting and eventually allowed him to move towards Schwitters-like collages, mixing the word with visual art.

Even more surprisingly, the 17 volumes consistently refer to one another. They are devised as one complex whole, building up to and complementing one another to form an impressively complete œuvre. Such long-sustained development and unity are rare, especially in the present poetic climate of fragmentation. Consequently, there is an unusual largeness about Reading's writing and the world depicted by him, one not often encountered in contemporary poetry. Indeed, the term "poetry" as it is still widely understood is perhaps not large enough to encompass his art, and it is thanks to writers such as Reading, and the publishers prepared to print their work, that contemporary perceptions of poetry are gradually gaining a broader base. (The adaptations of Reading's books into film, drama, music and photomontage attest to his appeal to other genres.)

Reading's *Collected Poems* map out an inconsolably sad, yet at times hilariously funny picture of England – and the world – in decline. They present an England that is deeply and disturbingly gruesome in its 'Post-coronation disintegration', but has 'a lot of dotty pleasantnesses about it as well', as Reading himself has put it. Within this framework, Reading's unblinkered tackling of serious issues such as madness (*Tom o' Bedlam's Beauties*), violence and

crime (*Diplopic, 5x5x5x5x5, Ukulele Music, Going On*), terminal ill-
nesses and dying (*C, Final Demands*), homelessness (*Perduta Gente,
Evagatory*), environmental catastrophe (*Evagatory, Last Poems*, and,
to some extent, *For the Municipality's Elderly* and *Nothing For Any-
one*) – in short, the collapse of nations, notions, and nature – as well
as his relentless focus on the foundations of life and society and on
the barbaric destructiveness of '*H. sap.*' have all extended poetry's
boundaries in dealing with global issues in a world gone morally,
ecologically and politically insane. Reading demonstrates that epic
subject matter and public traumas can be dealt with in the con-
temporary poetic medium, provided it is backed up by first-class
research and then employed with integrity, sensitivity and courage,
an original poetic imagination, and – last but not least – an ability
to transgress genres and the bounds of conventional sensibilities.

Reading's poetry faces human brutality and suffering head on
without sparing *any* of our – or his – sensibilities. This uncom-
promising confrontation with a savagely complex world has repelled
some readers – and to some extent Reading can empathise with that.
The versifying characters in *Stet*, for instance, who excel in escapism,
pretence, and pontification, may be exposed to the poet's ridicule –
other favourite targets are 'phoney-rustic bards', religious or polit-
ical fanatics, and 'Reps and execs in *Plastics* and *Packaging*' (*Going
On*) – yet at the same time they do warrant some measure of admir-
ation for finding solutions in a Mrs Gamp sort of way and for sur-
viving, albeit with their blinkers on. Unlike them, Viv in *Ukulele
Music* has the great virtue of 'Going On' without any fuss or self-
importance at all.

Thanks to this confrontation Reading has been called the *enfant
terrible* of British letters, the harshest satirist and most pitiless ob-
server of a decaying nation, and the 'unofficial laureate of grot Eng-
land'. While those descriptions are to some extent justifiable, they
are too narrow to do justice to the long development of Reading's
art. Two things need pointing out here.

First, Reading neither 'enjoys' nor elects to write about his tough
subject matter, but feels he is a kind of agent who has been drawn
into this area: 'anybody who lives in this country at this time would
be hard pressed to avoid grottiness... There is a dismayingly large
amount of unpleasant subject-matter about... I'm horrified by it,
moved in a negative sort of way.'

Second, under the surface of the contemporary social realism
there lies a more important and persistent existential basis. The
gruesome subject matter is not an end in itself, but presents itself

as a metaphor for the hopelessness and fragility of the human condition, as seen in the palimpsest of Homeric catastrophes, apocalyptic Anglo-Saxon visions, and the 20th century's own version of eco-nuclear self-destruction. Death-haunted like Beckett, Reading guides us through man-made wastelands so as to look our doomed destiny straight in the face and to confront the void of transitory, anonymous existence. He bombards his readers with atrocities, yet himself defies Medusa's gaze in the end – looking steadily at evil without freezing to flint is a true achievement. As Reading has remarked, 'If you want art to be like Ovaltine, then clearly some artists are not for you; but art has always struck me most when it was to do with coping with things, often hard things, things that are difficult to take.'

In building up an eschatological vision of contemporary life threatened by extinction, a vision both bleak and deeply humane, Reading's harrowing art aspires to nothing less than a distilled elegiac epic of our time while engaging in a heroic gesture of resistance, of non-acquiescence with the very destruction it predicts. The destruction, of course, is also seen to strike at Reading's art itself. The final, apocalyptic maelstrom predicted in the very first volume (*For the Municipality's Elderly*) is already brewing in the central section of *Ukulele Music*, and by *Evagatory* it is dispersing Reading's 'disbound *Collected Works*'. In *Last Poems*, in which Reading refers back to his whole œuvre, the very pages are eroding – and a fascinating literary journey is brought to a stringent conclusion.

This journey has moved smoothly through three phases. In Reading's first two full-length books conventional subject-matter was treated in unconventional ways. In *For the Municipality's Elderly* (1974) with its exact setting in time and place, Reading discovered symbols of the Human Condition in natural phenomena such as ageing and decay, thus finding an eschatological angle and striking a characteristically elegiac note. In *The Prison Cell & Barrel Mystery* (1976), a funny book on loving the right person at the wrong time, there emerged a wry humour and a recognisable voice, as well as a gift for formal organisation. Subsequently, in his deceptively simple third and fourth books (*Nothing For Anyone*, 1977, and *Fiction*, 1979) Reading indulged in formal acrobatics, creating Chinese-box worlds, satiric oddities, and intelligent anecdotes, incorporating and inventing 'found' material and feeling his way towards his future array of devices and themes – 'the Big Issue'. In *Fiction*, Reading also clears the way for more serious engagement by performing the fashionable 'death of the author' in an entertainingly unfashionable way, tongue-in-cheek. Aiming to write about what readers could empathise with, Reading first did away with the confessional mode of *For the Municipality's Elderly* and then eliminated the personal 'I' altogether, methodically 'killing' a character called 'Peter Reading' (and throwing in a few more deaths, just to stress the point). The next, thematically more focussed volume, *Tom o' Bedlam's Beauties* (1981), presents in a fractured way the fractured fates of perishing inmates of an asylum, strewing clues like a detective story in sharp images and an appropriate, original, taut structure. Its successor *Diplopic* (1983) also combines fun with horror and was given the label 'comedy of terrors'. It is Reading's first *tour-de-force*: the theme of double vision is masterfully executed in a succession of companion poems, all of which are parts of one bizarre narrative. *5x5x5x5x5* (1983) is an extension of the numeric poem '10x10x10' and works like a 5-act *dramolett*; it is also an intermezzo and a warming-up exercise for the masterpiece *C* (1984), which is, strictly speaking, not poetry as it consists of 100 mainly prosaic 100-word units.

Completely different, but equally outstanding is the sequence *Ukulele Music* (1985), which merges four disparate narrative strands and, along with *C*, *Going On* (1985), *Stet* (1986), and *Final Demands* (1988), marks the self-assured mature phase, in which Reading dealt with serious issues in highly sophisticated forms and structures. While in the early works narrative and drama were favoured, Reading now moved closer towards the lyrical or musical modes. In *Perduta Gente* (1989), a powerful rewriting of Dante's *Inferno*, Reading found himself using among other things the Old Testament prophets' voice. It was closely followed by the pamphlet *Shitheads* (1989), the second intermezzo and a translationese exercise combining translations of Catullus with his own poems on 'unsatisfactory people', as Reading puts it.

In the following year he had to endure a massive writer's block, but eventually completed the long valedictory – which had announced itself in *Final Demands*, Reading's most writerly book, which tries to decipher the runes of mortality and 'all things written' – in *Evagatory* (1992) and *Last Poems* (1994). The translation of 'life to lingo' is one of the themes of *Evagatory*, too, in which the poet's *persona* goes on his last odyssey, eventually wanders away, and, after a chilling account of both the inescapable force of *weird* and man's inability to learn, disappears forever, leaving only the echo of his voice in *Last Poems*.

This extraordinary enterprise is achieved among other things by the use of a prodigious array of artistic devices. Although the unified nature of his œuvre does not allow for endless variation,

Reading manages not to go over the same ground twice. In his technical skills he displays both incomparable ingenuity and virtuosity. He has a talent for eavesdropping and is a great mimic of a wide variety of registers from vernacular to posh, of sociolects, dialects and specialist languages. His use of the most varied tones, moods and masks is accompanied by bold, inventive formal structures and an abundance of accomplished, unorthodox metres of multiple provenance. His exuberant *dramatis personae* – from skinhead and ex-army to palaeontologist, char-lady and drunken bard – comically represent a Dickensian panorama of a richly stratified society, forming a cast of characters who recur throughout most of his books. The areas of knowledge displayed reveal widespread interests and considerable erudition. Readers of Reading are provided with insights into ornithology, oenology, palaeontology, astrology, medicine, the nautical profession and – above all – metrics. The material drawn upon and incorporated is at times very unusual – anything can fuel Reading's imagination, be it a wedding list, an 18th century recipe, or a medical dictionary. The ingredients of his art are so wide-ranging that before us arises a most vividly imagined world. Anybody reading Reading in the next century – assuming the existence of readers and books despite Reading's morose prognosis of 'mutated arthropods' – will encounter a stratigraphical slice of our epoch, studded with relics and signs of a past culture (from Aldermaston to Zimbabwe), of the end of the 20th century, maybe even of our civilisation.

This is all rendered with ferocious, passionate intensity in a poignant, idiosyncratic style. It is marked by a distinctive, energetic use of language, by a Swiftian rage counterpointed by a coolly classical, distanced stance, by an infectious and grim sense of humour, and by a satiric prophet's voice which is vigorous, anguished, courageous, unillusioned, sardonic and, at times, utterly disconcerting: it is instantly unforgettable.

Last but not least, much of the books' appeal lies in the fact that while Reading has got better with each successive volume and the language has grown increasingly dense and elliptical, his art has remained accessible and unpretentious all the way through. The keys to comprehension reveal themselves best if the books are read chronologically. Additionally, while Reading may cover a lot of ground, he has no time for spiritual speculation. His no-nonsense outlook never leaves the realm of secular common sense, thus also appealing to those readers who tend to favour the normally less ethereal world of prose fiction.

This said, it has to be stressed that the *Collected Poems* do not make for easy reading. They are an aesthetic, emotional and intellectual adventure in which the reader encounters a great number of unsettling experiences: besides being entertained and amused, we find ourselves baffled, provoked, exhilarated, distressed, and exhausted. Ultimately, though, we can be moved by the bleak nihilistic comfort of affiliation, of not being alone in the void. It is a grizzly, hard-won kind of support, but all the more honest and lasting for that.

Reading has received numerous literary prizes, among them the Cholmondeley Award (1978) for his first three full-length books of poetry, the Dylan Thomas Award for *Diplopic* (1983) for its 'combination of comedy, intellectual inventiveness, fantasy and energy of expression', the Whitbread Prize for Poetry for *Stet* (1986) and – in America – the highly prestigious Lannan Literary Award (1990) for 'writing that is critical and questioning, and that calls attention to essential humanistic values in imaginative and skilful ways'. As well as this *Collected Poems*, four of his books – *The Prison Cell & Barrel Mystery*, *Tom o' Bedlam's Beauties*, *Diplopic* and *C* – were Poetry Book Society Recommendations, *Perduta Gente* was a PBS Choice. He has also written and illustrated a children's book (*Rana*, unpublished), some 100 reviews, a few essays, and a handful of commissioned commentaries on his poetry.

After a controversial start, with heated discussions in the literary press about 'poetic' subjects, language and taste, Reading's reputation in Britain has grown steadily. He was included as a key poet in Bloodaxe's recent best-selling anthology, *The New Poetry*, and several critics have started to examine his art in close detail. Internationally, Reading's books have received immediate critical acclaim, especially in Australia and the USA. However, the utterly inadequate entry on him in the recent *Oxford Companion to 20th Century Poetry in English*, for instance, shows that his reputation is not yet entrenched in all quarters of the literary establishment.

Additionally, one of the factors which has hindered Reading from becoming known to a wider readership – apart from the hit-and-miss state of poetry reviewing – has been that most of his books have been out of print for years. This *Collected Poems* will remedy this unfortunate situation. It presents a desirable new starting-point for the public and critical attention Reading has always deserved.

Born in Liverpool in 1946, Reading developed a keen interest as a boy in ornithology, science and Natural History, which in his books all help to maintain 'a sensible distance' from the human cause, as he puts it. Exploring these subjects, he grew concerned about environmental damage long before it became a public issue. His other early preoccupation was with painting and literature: he wished to become a kind of artist himself, and wrote Keatsian poems (in flawless metre) which appeared in the school magazine and which he himself describes as 'execrable attempts about capital punishment or spiders' webs bedecked with dew'. Still in his teens, he trained as a painter at the Liverpool College of Art from 1962 to 1967 and started writing seriously at the same time, unimpressed by the pop culture going on around him. Similarly, today he does not feel much affinity with his contemporaries; his favourite reading is the 18th and 19th century novel.

Asked to name 'influences', Reading surprises many by mentioning the heroic diction and magniloquence of Old and Middle English poetry, which he read as a student (having come to admire Auden and Eliot as a matter of course before). His favourite poets are Gerard Manley Hopkins, Robert Frost and Edward Thomas for their precise observations of and unmawkish attitude to nature, for their metrical formalism, and – the last two – for their 'unassuming humanism'. All of these features figure prominently in his own writing, albeit in a completely metamorphosed framework.

Even more important for his own poetry was H.B. Cotterill's 1911 translation of the *Odyssey*, which found an accentual equivalent to classical hexameter and managed to combine the formal with the conversational in a vigorous, fast-moving way. The latter became one of the more well-known characteristics of Reading's style and the former the basis of ever more complex metres. As early as *For the Municipality's Elderly*, his first full-length volume (which is, unlike all the other books, metrically rather loose), Reading intuitively favoured dactyls – thought to be unsuitable for the English language, which is supposedly iambic -- on which he later built his falling cadences.

Still, in the next seven books he undertook a resourceful detour into the vast repertoire of metrics, done for the sake of reader-oriented variety and exercising his own virtuosity. The option of *free verse* was almost instantly dropped, as Reading did not wish to 'waste' any usable medium in the condensed art of poetry. Instead, he explored the possible functions and effects of stressed, accentual, and syllabic metres, of prose as well as concrete and visual elements.

The most frequent starting-points were iambic, dactylic, or trochaic trimeter, tetrameter, and pentameter, 3- to 6-stress-metre as well as alliterative Anglo-Saxon metre and triple metre, presented at first in irregular stanzas but, as time went by, in more specialised forms: quatrain, septenary, quatorzain, ballad, prose poem, *dramolett*, crossword puzzle, dramatic monologue, riddle, song, tanka, haiku, catalogue verse, Georgic, acrostic, *ubi sunt* poem, limerick, villanelle, Sapphic, tétramètre, Adonic, Choriamb, hymn, and numerous kinds of sonnets, with the tone ranging from *light verse* to *elegy*. He also invented a new kind of metre which works numerically (as in '10x10x10', '5', or *5x5x5x5x5*) as well as new stanza and poem patterns (see the 'Super Tanka' and the 'Japanese sonnet' in *Diplopic*).

Having touched on the elegiac distich in *C*, Reading returned to the *gravitas* of the dactyl-spondee beat in the next book and built it up to develop his own resonant cadences of elegiac distichs (*Ukulele Music*), Alcmanics and Alcaics (*Going On*), and a new combination of Alcaic with distich (*Stet*). They were 'the right kind of music for me', as Reading found. In the later works, many variations on these occur – eventually fragmented and dispersed in the end. Reading's metrical structures are anything but arbitrary: all have recognisable aesthetic tasks to fulfil, derived from their inherent potential. Above all, the elegiacs are the most appropriate form for Reading's theme of wholesale elegy.

In art, Reading was interested in the early cubists and abstract expressionists (see the 'cubist' poems in *Fiction*), while the 'combines' and 'readimades' of Rauschenberg, Jasper Johns and Jim Dine inspired his later use of 'found' material within a mosaic structure, allowing him to incorporate anything that was sufficiently important or pertinent. (They may also have triggered the elimination of introspection and the artist's own *persona* from the work of art.) The mosaic structure itself (emphasised by the lack of poem titles and even, in the original editions, of pagination in the later books) is partly a B.S. Johnson inheritance (*The Unfortunates*), but achronological arrange-ments are also a good way of keeping things moving. As Reading says, 'few enough people read poetry, and I don't want to bore the ones who do'.

Furthermore, Reading's work can be seen in the context of the literary strand of English pessimism, which according to him includes 'Henry Francis Lyte, Gibbon, Hopkins, Dickens, Smollett, Hardy, Wells, Waugh, Eeyore, Auden, Fuller, Larkin, and Drabble', and which derives from 'a congenital English pessimism, an English tendency to self-denigrate, the actual English experience of loss of Empire, and, arising from this last, all the connotations suggested by such a fall as had been delineated by Gibbon as early as 1776. [...] We register our own degeneration when we observe external decay, and view our personal disintegration as a metaphor for universal entropy.' His own substantial contribution to this literary line makes some renowned pessimists look like sandboys. However, incongruous as it may seem, Reading's nihilism is modified: by, on the one hand, sheer good fun and an albeit beleaguered enjoyment of life in these interesting, challenging times, and, on the other, his heroic metrics and attitude. His tender love of England – 'devenustated but yet, even though feculent, *ours*' as he says in *Stet* – is a further counterbalance. Sometimes it verges even on nostalgia, as in the antithetical structure of *Stet*, suspended between an elegy and an encomium of England.

From all this it should become clear that – while Reading's books are entirely original and partially innovative – his artistic method is eclectic. Drawing on the tradition of English pessimism, Reading uses in his own way any device that suits the artistic aim of a particular book: straight narratives, socio-political reportage, drama, lyrical or musical pieces, prose, classical metres, 'found' and pseudo-found material, elaborate fantasies, concrete poetry and visual elements, collage, modernist elements, 'postmodern' meta-fiction games. No single one of these things should be taken for the whole picture – it is, for example, misleading to call Reading a social realist or 'postmodernist'. His eclectic poetic merely corresponds to his own (and, indeed, everybody's) collated nature, and he has made his books transparent enough for careful readers to discover the eclectic old-fashioned traditionalist that he is ('it is just the way that I operate').

Old-fashioned is being a moralist for essential humanistic values with a generous love of the species and a Wellsian desperation at its lost potential. Old-fashioned is also the subordination of artistic considerations to the fundamental moral outrage and humanistic concern – a fact that Reading 'hides' by means of various artistic devices, e.g. by introducing numerous 'stances', 'masks' or 'personae' into his work so as to avoid becoming bad art or confessional in the name of a good cause. Again, it would be misleading to take those stances at face value and not to see them in the context of their respective functions, as has happened in the complaint that Reading wrote 'voyeuristic' poems. Only taken together do the numerous stances give the full, 'democratic' picture; they create tension and variety; they are, in the final analysis, fractured fictional-isations of the author's voice, which wants to be identified, found, and to have the last word.

These 'ground rules' for reading Reading are authoritatively established in *Fiction* through to *Going On*, sometimes explicitly in Reading's comments on both his art and his critics as in *Ukulele Music* ('Too black and over the top, though, is what the Actual often / happens to be, I'm afraid. He don't *invent* it, you know'), sometimes artistically coded as in the sly poem 'Opinions of the Press', which ironically culminates in the ridiculous question *'but am I Art?'* It may appear strange that misreadings have occurred of this writer who takes such great pains to make his artistic methods transparent, but this may just be evidence of Reading's success in 'rattling the cage' with his ferocious treatment of hurtful subject-matter. Art, he insists, does not mean you must not touch on certain things; nor is Art the raw material, however offensive the latter may be.

Nonetheless, beside the anger, dismay, and outrage there is an iota of relish as well, introducing a slight ambiguity. Reading admits to it in *Diplopic* by quoting Graham Greene ('there is a splinter of ice in the heart of the writer'), and he explains it by the need to provide a certain amount of frisson for the reader, and – because nothing can ever be *done* – the wish to 'embrace humanity with all its malodorous defects', as is exemplified at the end of *Going On*. That apart, 'we all have a lack of sympathy, or we wouldn't be able to tick over. We're spared real grief by the impersonality of most affairs.' So he proceeds to make it hurt again.

After his studies Reading abandoned painting because he found writing more articulate in the ways that interested him. Almost immediately his poetic career was launched on Radio Three by George MacBeth, who recommended Reading's first Outposts pamphlet (*Water and Waste*, 1970) to Anthony Thwaite, who sub-sequently published it in its enlarged form (*For the Municipality's Elderly*) with Secker & Warburg in 1974. Single poems appeared over the years in *Encounter* and *Poetry Review* but mainly in the weekly *Times Literary Supplement*, since Reading's poems were written in quick succession and he preferred to see them printed in a multi-disciplinary context.

After a brief spell of teaching Art at a Comprehensive School (1967-1968) and then at his College in Liverpool (1968-1970), Reading moved to Shropshire and, aged 24, got himself what he terms 'an honest job' working mainly as a weighbridge operator in an agricultural feedmill, first described in 'New Start'. Not inclined 'to mix with the *literati*', as he says, he preferred a job 'which is still in touch with some kind of reality.' It also gave him knowledge of a specialist working area which he found useful for his writing, as well as meeting 'ready-made *dramatis personae*' and hearing the 'continually mutable demotic, [the] rich Rabelaisian linguistic inventiveness' which he encountered there. Also, he was able to save his intellectual and creative energy for writing after and before work, although the strain eventually made itself felt. Neither fitting in there nor in the literary circles suited him fine, but Reading welcomed a break as a writer-in-residence in Sunderland (1981-1983), where 'they gave me $2^1/_2$ years and I wrote $2^1/_2$ books' (*Diplopic*, *C*, and *5x5x5x5x5*, respectively).

After 22 years at the mill Reading was sacked in 1992 for refusing to wear the new company uniform (which the media found more newsworthy than his poetry); upheaval had to be endured in his private life, too. 'Jobless, bereft of home, skint', like the poet in *Perduta Gente* three years before, he escaped to Australia, where his *Last Poems* were 'found' by John Bilston (an earlier pseudonym). He now lives in Shropshire again.

One of the reasons why Reading's books remain fascinating on re-reading is that they hinge on a series of paradoxes. His use of the oblique stroke, for example, with respect to humankind- 'love it/ loathe it' – is a bitter joke that maintains tension throughout the oeuvre. More importantly, antithesis is the only structure that can possibly hold the explosive contents together. As Reading announces in an (Alcmanic) epigraph, 'Just Going On remains possible through the/ slick prestidigital art of Not Caring/Hopelessly Caring'. Turning suffering into art is both morally dubious and morally desirable; at the same time, it is Reading's own personal way of coping. As Reverend Wolly puts it in *Going On*: he – badly – translates Alcman and Alcaeus to 'lighten/ some reader's heart, as my own is disburthened/ daily engaging in, if futile, harmless/ little unhurtful things'. This particular antithesis generates all others.

First, there is the combination of classical (in his case, heroic) metres with the language of the gutter and low subject-matter. The formal and demotic in Reading's language correspond quite simply to 'the dignified and bestial in behaviour', as he told one interviewer. Second, the knitting together of a detached and a personal voice (most openly in *Diplopic*) is interesting in itself, but also a means of keeping the hopelessly Romantic impulses of the poet in check through an abstracted Protean stance. Besides, sometimes choosing to write (like Addison) as a 'Spectator rather than as one of the species' heightens both poignancy and credibility on the one hand, and is an expression of impotence on the other. Third, the tension between Reading's pronounced Englishness and his desire to be global and non-parochial has resulted in a colourful and richly imagined world while producing a distinctly national epic. Fourth, the strong elegiac strain is effectively counterpoised by fine, shy, and very personal celebrations of food, wine, nature, and love – 'Only a troubled idyll now possible'.

The peak of the paradoxes, though, is Reading's sharp self-aware-ness and self-irony as regards the futility of his art: 'verse at the best of times/ chunters to insubstantial minorities'. Continually discussing the irrelevance of his Parnassian obsession in his poems, he keeps on perfecting them, casting doubt on both positions. This Beckettian persistence, if it wants to avoid repeating itself, must eventually be followed by the poet's retreat into his cranium, his muted evagation away from this world. With the publication of the pseudo-posthumous *Last Poems*, it finds its dignified resolu-tion in the ensuing 'Sibelian silence', the stance of ending things once and for all.

ISABEL MARTIN

Isabel Martin was born in 1962 in France, and grew up in Germany. She read English and Russian in Kiel, Cambridge, and Moscow, and has worked as a university lecturer, translator and interpreter. She now lives in a small village in the Rhine-Moselle area with her English husband and two young children. In 1994 she completed a prize-winning 550-page doctoral dissertation called *Das Werk Peter Readings (1970-1994): Interpretation und Dokumentation* for the University of Kiel. Her critical study of Peter Reading is forthcoming from Bloodaxe Books.

FOR THE MUNICIPALITY'S ELDERLY

(1974)

Fall

All engines cut out and snow made the birds dumb
stiffened and stuck in postures of sex,
and half-built nests were vacated to fill
like sailors' kit bags with feathers
and fell to the ground.

And where they were left to drain, the plates
froze in the night, and we found in the eerie
overbright morning that rhubarb leaves
had crusted the window.

The Goyt, already heavily burdened,
growled with the extra load and the weir
glowed white, and the groin of the bridge was pummelled
so that we feared it would not hold,
though it did, the sluice.

And those at the bank and the corner store
were that peculiar brand of politeness
that only climatic extremes,
or a war, produce.

Embarkation

Something today evokes (it may just be
the smell the grass makes stewing in the heat,
the sun illuminating crevices
I had not dreamed all winter still existed,
or possibly that undefined misgiving
I felt then and feel always underneath
the merely surface-pleasure summer brings –
a sense of somehow growing over-ripe)
a summer ending and a country halt.

Those in the sulphurous carriage were the same
as those who go unknown to business daily,
walk always clockwise aimless round the deck
until the plank is lowered and they file
into that city, on the other side,
of smoke and pimpled dummies and debris.
Odysseuses bound daily to commute
with rolled umbrella briefcase and dark suit.
And I have been among them on the quay,
placed pennies, at the turnstile, on our tongues.
I joined the train of lobster-pink old age.
Weeds prised the platform, where you waved, oblique.
The day was hot and stewed grass filled our lungs.

Earthworks

Earth oozed released, with a withdrawing foot
eased out like a deliciously oiled piston,
a smell of roots appeasingly primeval.
My father's bait-tin twenty years ago
locked-in the same lush juicy muskiness
and, opened recently, effused
all of the scent of bankside stoups
and gluten ferns and mud squeezed and flag crushed.
A fumbled pirouette in zipping-up
resulted in lost balance, and the ridged
and deep-fossed scoops and dykes of Caer Caradoc
rose tuberous and passed me overhead.
The best part of two thousand years ago,
effing and blinding, wet, and humping soil,
some grubby and regretted sad precursor
paused, so I like to think, sniffed, peed and pondered,
juggled with some half-glimpsed experience,
tripped, dropped it, and frustratedly rejoined
the mute pursuit of anonymity.

Plague Graves

We knew nothing of their existence before
you shewed us the other day five wrinkled
knobbly old and enormous fingers
tied down with heather roots tight to the moor;
and they, being buried three hundred years
ago, knew nothing about us, but neither
party's existence was any way less
for the other's ignorance of it.

                    To see
the same future waiting and still to continue
seems our most noble attribute, though
I suppose we secretly hope for some permanent
monument left of us, some recognition
by those coming after. No chance. Sheep maul
beyond recognition alarmingly quickly
the sandwich-paper memorials left
by charabanc trippers, dissolving all tangible
trace of us.

                    When the world ends and space-age
picnickers freeze to flint or melt or
asphyxiate or simply, no longer able
to read the already eroding incision,
just think five slabs have rather aesthetically
fallen above Gorse Hill, the result will
undoubtedly be the same in the final
analysis – no one to know them, extol them
or give them permanence in the now prevalent
sense of fame; and their mark will be not
in palpable stone but that they were once,
walked here, and did wonderful things.

Brabyns Park

The only permanence is, I suppose,
in having been – and whether known or not
to others, hardly enters into it.

Brabyns, for instance, in a local way
had, evidently, stature of a kind, –
landowners – little known though much outside
the district, even less now that a further
couple of hundred years obscures the name.

Scrub and unlevel rubble occupy
where the hall stood. The one real monument,
it seems to me, is that they occupied
it once themselves. Planned redevelopment
in coming years will crush all that remains:
litter of little stones sliced thin, incised
with Chang and Cani Fidelissimo,
long ago ghosts with ghosts in a ghost language;
the buttressed wall of orange biscuit-like
dry bricks, crisp, friable, flaking with each night's
juddering into gear outside the dead
still ornamental garden it encloses.

My wife and I are no less for the fact
he and his, similarly occupied,
watched skeletons disintegrate towards winter
across the pond, knew nothing and cared less
about us five or six generations past;

Qui Caecus et Senectute Confectus
reminds us of an earlier dynasty
no less alive albeit obsolete.

November 6th

Our lungs, too viscid to have diffused
the sulphur of last year's holocaust,
have merely ingested another's and groan,
and things intended have largely remained
unsaid for another year, and brown flakes
of mummy accompany now the papyrus
husks by early delivery dropped
on the lino. When, in such hours as these,
a perfidious cistern wakes me to stale
potato crisps knocking the lintel, crush
of retreating feet, and autumn, I
should prefer to have never, yawning, emerged
to a season so incontrovertibly gone
to decline.

Letter in Winter

Prologue

I hope I haven't given the impression
that married life is not my cup of tea,
or that my life is one long retrogression
(although there are times when it seems to be).
My wife and I, in fact, are both ecstatic;
but we are conscious, as we ought to be,
that peace of mind is flighty and erratic,
and individual values need revising
with every season. So it's not surprising
we should remember what the sceptic said,
hearing us glibly sing each other's praises –
affairs of heart are wont to move in phases,
will they be similarly eulogising
after the gilt has quit the gingerbread?

1 *November 5*

Nothing has happened since I wrote you last;
one or two poems thought of and abandoned,
my wife and I are still compatible,
the temperature has dropped a few degrees
and summer moves from this year into last.

I travelled home tonight through a Bosch landscape;
travellers moaned of prices and inflation
filth and negation and of no escape,
bonfires had been lit by the optimistic –
futile attempts at sulphurous purgation.

A million lights across the Cheshire Plain
shewed where a million meals were being made,
told of a million Aspros being taken
to ease rheumatics and to stop the brain
pondering the unbearable duration
from mid-November to the long vacation.

I started writing this the other night,
a bitter taste of pennies in my mouth;
my mood was changing with the failing light,
returning home by ferry and full bus
where workers spit the aloes taste of day
and talk of politics and flood and drouth
impassively to pass the time away
between departure and the terminus.

2 *Advent*

Nothing has happened that we did not know
yesterday or two thousand years ago.

Someone has been elected President,
the world is threatened by its own pollution,
though we care little of it where we grow
(reading of it in Sunday supplements)
detached behind the Situations Vacant.

Separate in thought though still co-resident,
my wife and I console each other nightly.
Not that we do not love each other dearly,
rather our love is interfered with slightly
by early rising and the sweaty mob
crowding the train each morning, and the dreary
nature of one's achievement and one's job.

We are awaiting yet another Christmas,
giving a last chance to a disproved theory;
above the streets the tawdry clowns grow tired,
impassive plastic faces losing patience,
regretting like tired gods what they have sired –
unctuous uncontrolled and unrequired,
a world fatigued and overweight and weary.

3 *Magi*

We have got nowhere since the time we started.

Do you remember in the failing light
stopping the car beside a curling beck,
the air as rich as honey with damp pines?
That was the last time that you saw me smile:
before the valley darkly slid from sight,
before the last of summer had departed
and silent bats spun underneath an alder
like some foreboding Alexander Calder.

That summer now is an annoying speck
causing an irritation in the eye.
The wind lays waste on Corporation piles,
crossing the street takes longer with each day.

Perhaps continuing will be no worse
than struggling across a busy street
giving assistance to an ageing wife;
slightly suspicious of the men we meet
on morning trains, who nod and slyly give,

crouched in dim corners of the smoky car,
a knowing wink behind the *Morning Star.*
If so then we must owe a debt to life,
and I suppose our payment is to live.

Baigneur

Unlike those in the Turkish Bath of Ingres,
pneumatic, poised to take off from the water,
the weightlessness in this reflection
lies in a different quarter.

Marat Assassinated by
David is much more fortunate,
having a quasi-Grecian torso,
(ever-so-slightly poncily
contorted in an heroic twitch)
than this deflated pachyderm
posing before a looking glass
counting up the bath towel stripes
like the seconds left before lift-off.

Archimedes-like it stirs
the pumice and the sponge, observes
the change a body undergoes
submerging for a third encore –
displaced, with not at all the sort
of buoyancy in Bonnard baths,
or in the hydrogen-balloons
of Renoir Baigneuses; more the sort
of unconvincing weight portrayed
in stiff fish in a minor nature morte.

Chez Vous

Something in you unnerves me not a little,
though I concede that you are very nice,
already you are on nodding terms with time.
Sprinkle your baths with rheumatism salts.

In spite of lithographs by twenties artists,
yellowed, but quite well-known and much admired,
and omnipresent literary persons
daily enacting derrière-garde play-ettes,
and over-zealous musical occasions,
a smell of dust and doubt pervades the hall.

Your Morse Code fingers on a full ash-tray,
and muffled noises from an upstairs room,
transmit with unimaginable gloom
unspecified frustrations and regrets.

Not to disturb the peace, an ormolu,
turned in disgrace, its face against a wall,
hammers, with angry metronomic knocks,
beats to the bar in allegretto time.

I dare not breathe in case my breath disturbs
your pressed-transparent mummy forms of brown –
the fossils of a lifetime's weed collection.

Reverberant (*allegro ma non tanto*)
your chorus echoes from your evening bath:
evenings are drawing-in quite quickly now.
The alcove window, where we sip dry sherry,
affords hermetic vision of a world
gone to decline. I call her Darling still,
she calls me Sweety though we have passed sixty.
Our son is taught by Mademoiselle Boulanger,
and plays delightfully. (*Diminuendo*)
we can afford a girl to do the chores,
we can afford to spread our butter thickly,
we have decanters of Sauternes for plasma,
and love-fired central heating for chill evenings
which, even now, are drawing-in quite quickly.

Severn at Worcester

Under Worcester the Severn, grown churlish, reflects
the Cathedral shattered today, the high column
scattered; the end of thirteen hundred
years of Christianity here.
Before that, Penda perhaps watched his Mercian
world shake in similar humour, shiver
across the same surface – swans glutting his vision
of civilisation in pieces inverted,
thinking it bits of bad bread.

None of that remains, the river deadens
everything – even the pointilliste stipple
of green on syrup buds browns in this water.
This spring seems the end of an era.

Following flood the reflux deposits
incongruously with plastic and rubber
a dredged sparrow gibbeted four feet over
the water pinned to a willow, and under
our feet remains of our own throwaway
society, thrown away, bleached bones
and bits of a thousand fractured monuments.

Appeasing to leave behind some record
of what our achievement was, provided
someone remains to read it. Watergate
marks with plates screwed into eroding
portals the heights and wastes of centuries'
deluges. All that remains of eights
is spray pounded into white powder wafted
a second, the surface crinkled a moment
and then reverting to flawed glass, clap
of blades re-echoed between black banks before
drowning, before they lose way to the tow.

Had we not been here to see it, their passing
would be no less a reality; Penda
would still have endured no less an existence.

May we then, in the event of our general
annihilation, regard as our forte
our once existing unknown to any,
our permanence and achievement a matter
of individual conscience – our handful
of plastic curlers and rubber-goods transience
lost to remain unwitnessed after
a deeper already gathering maelstrom.

Raspberrying

Last sun ripens each one, through rubicund, black
then each rots. Lines are tight with late swallows,
oak rattles leaves icicle-brittle...

A bit neo-pastoral, one will admit,
but then something conspiring to make decay more
than the usual end of a season makes Nature
itself as anachronistic today
as a poem about it.

Yet one feels almost justified still to acknowledge
the deeper reflection of, albeit hackneyed,
the Human Condition in Nature (reduced
as she is from the nympho once over-extolled
for ad-nauseam cyclic fecundity, to
today's stripped-bare and thorny old sod half-heartedly
whorily pouting a couple of blackening nipples).

Stills

A sepia plate of Greatgrandfather,
incorrigibly confident Victorian
(or, rather, blind to the contingency
of his empyrean Empire crumbling),
arm round his wife,
reminds me of us
reflected in the window of a train
flickering into the dark.
Though the frame is shaken at every point
and our edge is lost,
blind faith is manifest still in the brittle
inherited pose.
The only sound is that of a tambourine rubbed
in the empty restaurant car as cutlery rocks
on set deserted tables.

Stroboscopically jerking
on a white-flecked screen, suddenly
we find ourselves mummers in a Keystone Cops,
slithering on oiled ice.
Even rooks are soundproofed
in new nests become huge white muffs.
Muffled in our undignified
parabasis, a decorous
gesture still survives in us
who seem already flickering
stills from the silent era.

Early Closing

At the idle aqueduct, scribbled over with weed now,
Grandfather would find an abundance of animalcules
for his lens, stoop, and conclude 'an unneeded brief cycle'
were he alive.

Here a young couple asked me today
how far to the next place along the towpath
where they might veer to the shops on a fleeting visit.
Narcissistically I feel sorry for all those like them
persisting against today's predicted bad weather.
The forecast is levelled against them, the long-range is worse.

Corrugated tin sheet reports in a dribble of Morse.
The scarcely living are numerous now as the dead.

I would like to be with the Old Boy to swap specimens;
taking them magnified we would conclude the same.

A low from the north is levelled against those who come here
today for the shops or anything else, and besides,
it is Wednesday – everything worthwhile is already closed.

Nomenclator

Daily on the way to work
he calls the bus crew Charon
and murmurs *donna mia*
ch'io non perisca.

Climbing the stairs he calls a fight,
in the chalk-heavy air
turning him daily prematurely white,
and murmurs *donna mia*
ch'io non perisca.

He hesitates to call the dance he does,
immersing in bath-water drawn too hot,
death dance;
and calls his only child
his second chance.

When even sex has ceased to be sensation
he calls his marriage
mutual consolation
and, lying with his wife
without prowess,
calls the appalling sheets
a wilderness.

Spring Letter

1 *Calvary*

Since my *Letter in Winter* was written, over
a year has gone out of us. We have moved house
and are shortly to leave here for good; it seems sometimes
our time here has been too prolonged.

                      Today
on the Nob hunched over this black northern splatter
of chimneys, lapwings whip down like Stukas
spun in a vortex, an inch from the ground
pulling-out, urged on by instinct to love
(though it seems courting death – and the two are fused
on this dead spring day; all coming alive
too late at the end of a season).

                    A lamb,
joints stiff, brittle, jabs at maternal clogged fleece,
spattered red (which is ruddle but looks already
like blood and soon must be).

                More than a year
is dead in us since I last wrote.

2 *Good Friday*

We are contemplating departure even
as glycerite buds in a neighbour's pear tree
mark an irrevocable change
about to occur; we shall not see spring here again.
Accordingly, cresses and mint at the brink
of Brookbottom, juicily mulched, and an early
twist of wet fern crunched, stood on, a primed
coiled spring, have assumed the quality of
memorials though they are nascent as yet.

This Good Friday on Cobden Edge a huge cross
has sprouted up overnight, and pilgrims
celebrate now (the scarcely living
greeting the dead and the resurrected).
pray for a new beginning to come
from the sudden end of a season.

3 *Primavera*

Per me si va nella città dolente,

I still commute to Liverpool. On Mondays,
in the Department of Art History,
I index slides below the city street,
next to the central heating plant whose drone
deadens the senses, in a steaming vault
where my own sour smoke chokes me. Here the season
reaches me buckled, sieved through reinforced
opaque glass blistered with an uneven pox.
Transparencies float now before my eyes.

Next spring will find my life and work elsewhere,
greener and pleasanter, if it's not too late.
Nothing of me is likely to remain
among these records of two thousand years'
obsolete art, reduced, collecting dust.

A two inch square of Botticelli, held
up to the light, reveals a greener world
than I see daily or can hope to move to.

Aeschylus

There was a reason, though it now evades me,
why I should nervously wink at the sky.
Its bland crepuscularity pervades me,
though that can hardly be the reason why.

I read once as a child how a tragedian,
with tragic irony or will of fate,
met death by tortoise and short-sighted eagle
which mis-identified as rock his pate.

Who but perhaps an avant-garde comedian,
or Darwin postulating on board *Beagle*
on how the turtle's flippers were evolved,
could visualise the tortoise so insidious
as, first to take wing, then to get involved
with poets quietly in pursuit of grief.

I view all life now with grave disbelief,
find all on earth reptilian and hideous,
and Heaven sly, potentially perfidious.

Juvenilia

Little has changed; involuntarily
the Goyt still flows, brownish and throaty,
choked with smoke from the valley homes
where our like have decayed for generations.

Juvenilia, scattered now in the slack,
coil to the weir and are sucked under oil.
Traces of rainbow remain of loves
more turbid than ever before or since,
though far too desperately set down –
my being, believe it or not, at the time,
involved and wishing to commentate,
incredible now though it seems.

Politics too, less than half understood,
and a half-baked kind of philosophy.

But having found love I am left with nothing to say.
And I find, in place of Socialist leanings,
a ninety per cent misanthropy,
which once expressed gains nothing by repetition.

Thus, satisfactory poems have been,
through, first over-need, then through absence of need,
unwritten. And being has changed from the bore
of perpetually thwarted joie de vivre
to a sense of inert indifference.

The Goyt, from the overhang of this bridge,
changes in characteristic from,
on one side asthmatic but indisputable
life, to a moribund slack on the other
where, deeper, the undercurrent remains
towing a slack immobile body
of water and waste away involuntarily.

For K.J. (Aged 3)

'I don't want you not awake.'

I am fagged out at a time
when you find mild interest not
black significance in what
is happening around me.
We are sapped today and browned,
rind is crusty on ripe muck.

A horse eye squeezes shut,
discharging like grape-shot
flies from its rim, then rolls
nigger-minstrel-like.

Falling, dreamt of near to sleep,
or gnats pestering the tender
abscess prompts a shudder,
ripples a length of flank
(as love used to, by the way).

Do not be surprised, KJ,
to find me dropped off early
on a sickly hot July
afternoon (though really I
never seemed to get warmed up)
on a lawn cropped sickle-height
cold, a bottle at my head,
and the foxglove that you pulled
an extended soggy comma
coyly dangling at my end.

Chiaroscuro

Reminiscent of Grandfather photogravured,
impenetrable, on guard, an alarmingly
nondescript chiaroscuro in brown
confronts me from unbiased uncompassionate
depths of a butt in a wilderness corner.

Immured in a collar of steel, unremembered
by litters of unending progeny, seems
our mutual prospect.

                    But whereas the surface-
calm of the goon in the barrel is rippled
with frowns, the framed memorial (facing
a mirror) exhibits the Old Boy's commendable
talent for staring bald anonymity
straight in the face unperturbed.

Removals

(Not actually) written in dust on the rear of the van:

Living here has had its advantages I suppose
but we're tired of the place and the time has come to depart.
The Coal Board will make us redundant and pension us off.
You can stuff Conservation Year – let's get it over with quickly.

That rich as liqueur almost puke smell, distilled from a hollow
splattered with marigold wafers of sweltering butter,
is a pastoral souvenir – the closest we ever
can hope now to get to the ruined original.

And there's pus in the weir; where once a white cumulus froth
of cauliflowers boiled, there's a fetid and curdling slack
of turpentine slick clotting up with each new pollutant
in a piled scum of rainbow blown corrugated and poxed,

while the same goes on in our own intestinal tracts.
So it worries me now, I think, less than it used to to leave it –
I recall without envy an old snake tired of itself,
with the sound of fat fried, sloughing a palpable ghost

to remember it by on an earthworks whose builders are lost.
Will there be any tangible thing to remember us by?
I think not; but living with being anonymous
has almost equipped us to face leaving nothing behind.

Mnemonic

(for N.H.)

I will think of you in three ways: (1), at work,
having just done something or going to do it soon
but not at a given moment doing it,
plagued by amnesia and tribulations
like a birthday in the family forgotten
or another of your own too well remembered
or an in-tray plump with indigestibles
or the top lost from your Parker 51
or a ricked back. (2), and more the real you, painting –
or rather just about to paint or having
just primed a canvas, somnolent, adjourned
into the succulence of the studio chair.
(3), tragi-comic, through a glass
faceted like a hand-grenade,
gurgling anecdotes deliciously
with the sound of water when it leaves the bath,
having just bought or going to buy a round,
seeing about you us becoming slowly
satyrs and tenuous shadows gathering
for your committed final Bacchanal.

New Year Letter

You used Propertius once to preface
a ghost poem sunt aliquid manes
letum non omnia finit.

                              Should auld
acquaintance be forgot ... comes fizzing
out of the box like bacon frying.

A third of my life ago in a Liverpool
park at lunchtime in summer we followed
the Wye with dead stems through Herefordshire
in a fissure mapped in fired mud, a patch
that relieved an off-green prospect. Marvellous
things have occurred since then that can never
survive in a concrete sense.

                              The drawn
straws settled (and it was decided that I should)
at Ross. Now when I look at the map I seem
not far short of that end we envisaged
but sooner than I had thought.

                              If I die
tonight, I say to myself each bedtime,
what will remain is either the abstract
intangible fact of any anonymous
ghost's former being – millions of wonderful
things done, fun had, luscious and sour food
and drink savoured, wife wallowed-in, despair,
boredom and curious incidents – or
the limp parenthesis of this
in a palpable soft cover.

                              A speaker
crackles that history is that
which remains. This assumes historians.

In 1936 the dust of
Housman was brought to Ludlow and it
was requested it should be lodged within
the church. It was done. The place selected,
the north wall of the nave, the ashes
injected into the masonry, sealed
with a grouting of liquid cement. HIC JACET
A.E.H. is that which remains, while
his poems are not in the library here
today. But he did them (albeit a bit
Boy Scoutish) though we may not read them. And he
will remain the same when the church is dust.

So I hope (especially if my possessions
are lost or, the same on a larger scale,
if Conservation Year lets us down
or the planet poaches leaving none
or someone important's books are lost)
that history is what happened, known
or not.

       My best friends are fifty and seventy,
most of their lives being over. One keeps
his manuscript autobiography locked
in a safe against fire. The other will leave
two softbacks a hardback and one translation.
Neither will be any less miraculous
lives for the fact that their tangible remnants
hint at inadequate drafts of them.

               Next door
he died yesterday and the landlady whispered
it makes you think. She was wrong. I encountered
him on the stairs last week with a bag
of mince under neutral gaberdine
and it made me consider his history more
than when I was told the predictable – like
the unfunny punchline of some boring
joke.

If the broadcast was right, history
is a couple of wizened apples, an egg
(preserved in the washroom we shared by the hardest
frost of the winter that permeated
thick plaster the night he left), a suitcase
awaiting collection by relatives, in
the hall a knot of mistletoe blisters
over a barely started end
on the hatstand stubbed out blunt.

It cost him
ten new pence or two old shillings.
We all will be decimalised he told me
bearing his twist of wet plastic see-through,
bubbles and ducts of bruised ooze swollen
purple with pressure.

The wireless hisses
auld lang syne...we must leave something quick
if the broadcast was right. These decimalised
days one new year is worth twenty-four
of the old ones (in my case, and fifty or so
in yours I suppose) to make something durable.
Lof the Saxons called it – fame
in one's lifetime, the only way to combat
transience.

Fractional tuning commits us
to an historic stronghold where
vases above the fire which are Meissen
and heads the Seventh Earl slew which are bison
are the only transmitted memorials
of that ilk.

Devious thinking, however,
consoles in some measure one's sense of being
anonymous, makes for a kind of history
quite independent of human acknowledgement.

Outside your cottage we watched a star
fizzle and set in a mole fur sky.
Unobserved at Mount Wilson, still it remains
the single factor that altered all heaven
and earth to its present exactness and future
course.

        So perhaps what remains is our old years
preserved by being responsible for
the precise programming of other new ones.

Shadows perceptibly move round your cottage
and grow. Plum darkens odd humps in the lawn.
A family of nine who lived here leave no trace.
Above, Caer Caradoc darkens your shorter
afternoons with an umbra from earth heaped
less than a hundred generations
ago. What they left is unimpressive
compared with their having been here and left it.

For the Municipality's Elderly

Things here grow old and worn with untragic
logic.

        Sated we drowse supine
on a bench incised FOR THE MUNICIPALITY'S
ELDERLY.

            Withering limbs a long summer
smoulders in ashes.

                At evensong
spent faces from almshouse windows follow us
into the dusty column of late
afternoon oblique amber. Still there persists
a smile of attained appeasement in worn
grained skulls, streaked knobs of warm butter with no more
of life left in them, misericords.

50

Stubble is parched on a tumulus now
that when ripe was moist peach flesh. On top of us
coiffures of willowherb fleece puff their last
uphill.

In Castle Gardens fermenting
mulch in September, honey fumes throb
a mirage of clipped lobelia beds
where we loll and, ungrudgingly, limp with stooks
too long left on fields beyond Broad Street, brown
and burn out.

Duo

We seem to only at vacations
but all must return to our dusty origins
sometime.

My wife preceded me
last Christmas to ancestors, leaving the flat
a cold accumulation of ash,
the street a frozen xylophone. Through
a yellow net Lagorio's showed
a vista of tables for dinner, appalling,
all set for one – the worst was not
the prospect even of sleeping alone but
of facing that regular evening consumption
quite unattended.

Moss on the step muffled
bottles the milkman chimed me awake with
at grandparent's twenty years ago
to a desert of sheets and my mother's breathstopping
absence. Under umbrageous trees
in tweed; on crochet, an icon edged
with silver between a blue Victorian
glass and the ghyll-edge of bed, she seemed
everlastingly elsewhere. Mothballs were used
which smelt of delay and attempted impossible
preservation.

                    A gentleman
whose jacket whiffs of naphthalene dines
with dignity in the pub, his lapels
curled like claw-hammers testify
to life in continuous solitary,
and brings the two most active in
my own brief presence nearer dead.

Curfew

I have cut you the earliest snowdrops but they won't keep white
in the house where dust precipitates with your departure.

The hands are static. The clock and the power have cut out.
There is no guarantee of normal voltage resuming.

My laundry stagnates. There is little to nourish me here now.
My dead bottle thuds in the bin with the same dull clank
as the Curfew Bell has in the Garden of Rest at 8.

The greenhouse has shrugged, shucked-off algal scales to the earth.
Through the ribs, from anus to gape, worms greedily slide.
The curtain is drawn, I see you in that skeleton daily.
The delicate growths you implanted are turning to loam.

Wilks, over the sweetshop, circuits his uncurtained room.
In bottom gear, the bereaved man from work overtakes me,
pedals a shadow towards quarters newly unlit.

In the chip-shop, prattle is spitting with hot fat at all of us
('it's worst for the one that dies first – not just for the dying,
but because neither one wants to leave the other behind').

You may not be dead, Love, but only away for a week –
though, through that, the first part of the season here is quite from
          you
and I cannot cut and conserve it for you to return to.

Fossil

It seems difficult to believe (though that
was a season past and the air drugged
with pine and new bracken, the kid, barely fleeced then,
lolled in new growth, rucks of primroses)
this is the same place.

Seventy kinds
of fungus grow here now. There is more punk
than ever, this kindest winter (the Met. Office
tells us) of all our years. Too much
decays – insufficient dies.

Tonight
the uncurtained last house in town reveals
an Asian refugee without volume
flat in the box. We approach him in
as deep a silence beyond Dinham Bridge.
Here the Teme dies. Sonar blimp from the swimming-bath
echoes men drowning.

Each morning at milking
cows booze, snort grain in mangers deadened
with kibbled swedes and wait to exude but
tonight, at the last, mute beasts' tongues chafe troughs bare.

I cross the Tin Bridge this morning (spring
of a dead goose whose limbs belt the air but the body
seems stuffed) on the way to work and then
a gate with a stepping-stone pierced by fossil.

Too much time and pressure reduced
clay to this stone spiral from which
I have just descended, after dark
will return to.

Easter Letter

Palms are down on the chancel slabs,
hope for the dead is the week after next.

The castle gleams like roasting duck,
south-facing corners irradiate
nine hundred years. Forty or so
generations like us who have willingly
browned, flaked-dry here, steam from the walls
and nettled moat.

             In a month May Fair
will occupy Castle Square, but generate
only a sense of pending departure;
relics of sympathetic men
more palpably are distilled from this
angle of sun-douched Norman stone.

I fade through years to a fair with a schoolfriend,
quite beyond contact now, the Big Wheel
sickeningly revolves, we first glimpse
immortality – our insides
keep going for ever after our bodies
have stopped.

             A more terrestrial kind
of ghostliness than Easter means
I still believe in, different from
the declaration on the plaque
BY.ADAM.IN.TE.DVST.ILYE.
BY.CHRIST.I.AVE.TE.VICTORY.

Another irony, another
season; new flowers are in the font
and on new graves.

             The Almshouse inmate,
paralysed, is flyblown; blind
eyes from another life ascend
the dark tower of St Lawrence's.

Bats like black balloons released,
out of control, deflating, catch
aphids newly hatched to gorge
on the uncovered corpse. The hide
is worn-transparent, stretched-tight membrane
over frail bones against the moon.

Conveniently adjacent is
the Cottage Hospital. Three weeks
I have watched the patient in
the first floor left-hand window, as
at evening I return from work,
jacked-up prepared for visiting-hour.
Kleenex, hyacinth, Lucozade
are still apparent, the bed is bare,
crisp sheets are neatly creased oblique.

Turn the switch, join in the chorus
'what to do about it? – let's
put out the light and go to sleep.'

The Crucifix is now in High Street.

Spare us, good Lord, spare thy people
whom thou'st redeemed with thy most precious
blood, cried Solomon Eagle running
loose denouncing of judgement on
the City, in most frightful manner –
a pan of burning charcoal upon
his head, for the rest quite naked – through
White Chapel (1665
during another plague).

                On short wave
the Budget fizzles out to music
interference, ritardando,
pound in the pocket pound in the grave,
reduced death duty, ritornello.

The phone's still warm from some late caller
joined now with the flickering shadows
of other evening commuters returning,
tenuous, quiet, the other side
of the glass.

The evidence of men
vanished is thick in Deepwood Lane;
the hedge is split and pleached neat by
a ghost. No one remembers who
installed the boozey where beasts schnorkel
sweet molassed oat straw.

                    A crust
of lichen seals the lid on a former
curate of Pipe Aston under
his favourite yew. The list of vicars
since the church was built has filled
only one quarto sheet, congregations
are still here mulched in the cider orchard.
With apparatus for rolling and raising
heavy objects, a fat man in tails
converses with matron, opens the boot.

Eli, Eli, lama sabachthani?

Faithful and simpleton are singing
hope for the dead from this morning on.
Wipe the dust from the chocolate egg.
A human hip bone stirs on the pile
of strewn daffs in the Garden of Rest.

Almshouse

My routine passage lies between
almshouse and graveyard. The former side
holds one, with fish eyes starting to bloom,
who cross-checks, by withering looks at me
and an ear cocked up to St Lawrence's tower,
(each hour on the hour a reminder chimes,
each day one worn tune gives way to another)
the quantity left of diminishing light
as we make an advance on equinox.

The Conquering Hero chimes. She marks time;
and mine is measured by Klaxon, honk
of the future being throttled, I must
return from the world to dust at quarter-to.
Men's ghosts overdraw time at the mill,
clock-in late in the red. The hearses
rattle over the weighbridge – how much
they may carry is in the balance. On
an alloy stool towards late afternoon
I spin with, under me, coiled-round chrome,
legs belonging to one quite elsewhere.

Chromium tubes and tubes full of sand,
thick-gauge sand-coloured hose, the one
with the haddock eye from a wheelchair watches,
does not blink. With the sun three-quarters
down, the inscription over the door
is channels of shadow. Through the daisies
each impartially watches the other
crossing towards the other side.

St James's

On Holy Thursday cycling in the Lakes
I found St James's on a pewter hill
and force of habit rather than desire
carried me on towards the wrought iron gates.

The dusty Dunlops and the worn out brakes
of my Rudge leaning on the lake-stone wall
seemed more akin to Larkin than to me.

Some stones inside the musty porch were Saxon,
and there, beside the patent-leather Eden
simmering round St James's in Lent sun,
the sexton, one spring day digging a grave,
in 1898 unearthed remains
that proved to be of Viking origin.

The latest stone, marked 1968,
shews that the process is still going on.
I, in my turn, turned the worn rusting latch,
saw the inevitable Norman arch
and, near the font, some notes by Reverend Twigge
about the church and local history –
he was the rector here in nineteen seven,
in his place now is Geoffrey Dennison Hill.

I climbed the old steps up the Western Tower
(added about 1248) and found
barrows of sticks from jackdaw generations,
piled in a stook beside the swaying bell
eggs and dry feathers and winged skeletons,
and I descended into the chancel,
observing, not from interest but a sense
of having to have a sense of history,
the aimless woodworms' doodles in the roof.

The empty Player's *Weights* pack in the font
belonged to Betjeman, I have no doubt,
and there was Larkin's shilling left in trust
as payment for the Reverend Twigge's epistle;

but I was not there, just a cardboard copy
guiltily going through the motions of
what all day-trippers do before they leave,
replacing bike clips, lingering at the door
giving the closing latch a final twist,
consulting Twigge one final time before
turning from font to underground stone kist.

Mortimer Forest

All afternoon the drone of a saw has fanned
with resin over this bank of vibrating pines;
with each completed sever, falling an octave –
the one, only, sound of another human
in all dead, hot, black Mortimer Forest.

I have seen the place; clearing, sawdust, tarpaulin,
pipe-dottle, that is all, never the man.

If it stops now and I go there I will find,
to mark hard work for so long, long weeping ranks,
curtailed, seasoning in glutinous tiers,
and dust, dust red wood-ants perpetually sift.

Juncture

Where I work, a rural siding
breaks from the northern/southern route,
provides a parsleyed cul-de-sac
narrow-gauge alternative.

So strange to see you, whom I loved
ten years ago, flicker across
the gap in this abandoned cut
with red NO SMOKING triangles,
my still not-quite-extinguished flame,
with unmistakable reflex
shifting hair from brow to temple.

Spring has returned to me; you can't.

The life I led in your world, now
seems the slow death of someone else.
Memory returns without me.
Are you receiving me through steel
dolorous Inter-City lines?

Are my contemporaries dead?
Has drink or pot claimed Pom. and Baz.?
Mad Dawson who once shaved his head
rather than lose a ten bob bet –
severed, that pate recurs in dreams,
black puckered walnut soused in brine.
Mooj. with his eighth-rate lectureship,
rearguarding what new Ism? You
drowned when your scallop shell capsized
only last night in warm white-fleeced
Aegean, and I woke up stiff.

Decaying here at least is lush.
Stinkhorn festers each side of me,
parsnip wine last Christmas gave me
shrunk-tight granny-knot intestines.
We kill rats with crab-tree sticks,
we thread jackdaws on a blackthorn,
spike dead moles like finger-stalls.
Teddy is lynched on next door's line.

Wallflowers drench the air with syrup –
I recall St Philip's Garden
from the arched gate where it started,
coupled with a sad misgiving
that, whereas you never loved me
while I loved you, you might love me
after I had ceased to love you.

There you buried that world for me,
and its unreal population;
now your unexplained appearance
from the window of a train
at this distant country juncture
leaves behind a trail of sleepers
drawn out from infinity.

Combine

Being neutral, the first we see of it is its shadow
approaching, laying bare whole acres.

                                    The vast
departure is now irrevocably underway;
only telegraph wires are alive, the sky is empty.

Sap sinks from live limbs, the dead are shrouded with mauve
faeces of birds gorged sick on blackberries.

I seem to have been with you only an instant here;
idyllic becomes fearful grave silence as I awake
to you already arisen, the steady thresh
and much nearer shadow of the quiet harvester.

Burning Stubble

All stubble is being burned, a chiffon pall
is settling over round flesh-tint hills, it seems haunches
of supine bodies unbreathing after a fall.

We see them for the last time, all those men, their huge
efficient harvest; last light is pressing the panes.

Off the Teme at this season fog sinks us all, snuffs each
light in the low water-meadow out.

                                    We have grown
to expect these things here at this time (late harvest),
pyres, the extinguishing suck of mists
on September dusks, as we expect
winter thrushes in season and
the dark swift coming and going.

Night-Piece

Although ready to, I can't get to sleep yet,
detained by forty huntsmen galloping
all dressed black up an unfamiliar
lane, or clocking a ton in a sports job
steered by the wife of a friend. I sweat
curry powder, events of the day are reduced
to clipped rushes... off goes the Sprite with the blonde
whom I kiss goodnight as if for the last time.

We sit facing west towards evening, watch
England grow dark and disappear, swallow
two more finos and draw the curtains.
And then one more, to make up for lost time.

Ball claps bat. We're aware today
of perhaps our only achievement ever –
carrying on as if nothing was wrong (though
I kiss you tonight as if for the last time).

Turned earth, the empty trench, then we enter
among varicose alabaster knights
and petrified other Elizabethans.
The Great G minor Fantasia
knits an acoustic cobweb; however
curtains refuse to reveal the player
playing tonight as if for the last time.

Even our best friends' three-year-old daughter,
an Armageddon of pink ice-cream,
reminds me that there are too many of us.
Kiss her tonight as if for the last time.

Black in the face, gasping fish-out-of-water,
white palmed, white rim round mouth, baby gulps
Al-Jolson-like (Mammy Mammy Mammy,
a million miles for your smiles for the last time).

Latest computer forecasts inform us
in thirty years time she'll be gulping for real.
Top-up your larynx before they call Time Please.

The modern finale is molto vivace
...a pause...across fields to the chancel wafts
applause, a good man is run out at thirty.
Pick up his stump, hang it up for the last time.

Under the curtain the unrevealed player
(volles werk volles werk spun and woven)
cuts to a weird choreography done
by Clotho, Lachesis, Atropos,
circling the bed in infectious ragtime.

Lapse

Burrington tombs are cast iron;
hot-plates in summer, they scorch worms.
All that rises from them is mirage.
Once, late harvest broiled us, we saw blurred
two graves through vibrating air,
and beyond, palpable heat, nothing more.

In mid ascent from the orchard edge
a flycatcher stuck on air,

on the spire, the big finger, downpointing, lapsed,

then under it each cell resumed decaying
to only chemically recur.

Winter digests us, the crone yew drips.
Wind scrapes a dry oak leaf over a dead choir.
Now only foul gas drools from this organ.
Livid fur smothers an Old Testament,
big black dormant flies tremble in Genesis.

Horticulture

Thought nauseous by his wife, A. Barns, B.A.,
devotes himself entirely now to work –
the running of a Comprehensive School.
Though overweight and bald, in his heyday,
what with the war and Sandhurst and all that,
he must have seen a lot more life than me;
and, while headmastery is not my cup of tea,
I grant that chacun à son métier.

Thrombotic, he will soon be pensioned-off.
His favourite geraniums in their pots
are dry already on the study ledge
drip-fed with phosphate from a lead pipette.

Nil desperandum iterates the man
beyond despair already, while our own
policy's champion is his secretary –
daily, against all odds and horticulture,
administering Liquinure with care
on aphid's unavoidable injuncture.

Dead Horse

Not to be born is best, said Sophocles
(a second-bester with the rest of us).

When a close neighbour suffered her bereavement
she got quite good at doing watercolours
(striving for tolerable second-bests
may be to blame for all human achievement).

Not to be born is best, said Sophocles
(or, second-best, to pass the tedious years
devising therapeutic compensation).

With marriage (or at least the sexual act)
we have groped through darkness, if not without tears,
at least towards a sweaty consolation,
making our mutual best of a bad lot.

Not to be born is best, said Sophocles,
(the second-best is an abysmal bore)
a view which he would re-assert, I'm sure,
hearing the second-rate asthmatic wheeze
of this ephemeral trite Audenese,
the product of a brain long dulled and clogged,
the patter of a dead horse being flogged.

Dirty Linen

A wheezed staccato and hypnotic linen
unendingly whirled with a purling tub
in the coin-operated laundrette:

He's in the army now my eldest one
I pass the long days here and spend the evenings
Reading his brief once-weekly letters home
Now there is little to be done

Struldbrug is at the vet
Enduring distemper
His breathing is erratic
Only his decline is steady

Have you the time?
Already?
My wristlet watch is away for repair
The Sound of Music is at the Hippodrome
They say the priest has gone out of his mind
The guarantee said it was anti-static

Hope is A.W.L.
Hope is having choking fits
Hope has a fractured mainspring and has gone to the mender's
           until he can find the appropriate missing bits
Hope is an usherette with a broken torch
And there has been no hope at the vicar's ever since that
           unfortunate business of the chorister in the porch
(Now he is something quite high-up in Zen)

All our hope now is in our dirty knickers whirled without end amen

THE PRISON CELL & BARREL MYSTERY

(1976)

Early Stuff

I have been looking through his early stuff.

'You have,' he wrote of me in *Poster Girl*,
'the same too good to touch, too high to reach
qualities as that ad. girl, quite too much
to hope for. Your blouse wrinkles in the rain,
and where your heart is, underneath the now
transparent pink silk, re-appears the man
who you were stuck on last.'

                      In his *Au Pair*
'My now bare moon-beamed room is claustrophobic,
along the shore the last ebb churns. Tonight
I kiss your thin hand noting the blue vein
of Biro slowly crinkling in my hold
as I release burnt fragments to the reflux
leaving moist shale, an empty shell, and ash
of what you wrote unlovingly from France.'
That was unfair.
              We parted shortly after.

'A new-sawn stack of peeling birch fence poles
at ithyphallic 45 degrees
unheals a year's scar, resurrects this scene:
the sun streaming through branches in thin lines
pierces with shadows soft as velvet moles
the rind peeled back on piled lopped logs of birch,
a girl's hair deep and smelling of coal tar
shadows my face again. The sun is low.
Our shadows now are longer than we are.'
After *Umbrae* we patched things up.

                          'Re-linked
in the park palmhouse hot glass cranium,
temperature rises with each opening door,
tormented steamy ferns drip, your tights stick,
air clings to lungs like candyfloss. Outside
lovers are strewn like white stones on the banks
of the brown lake. I wither for your love.

It is as hot as Hell – ironically
this globe sustains a Bird of Paradise.'

Of course he cashed in when Grandmother died –
'The quack says there's no chance, meanwhile she sleeps.
The sloppy Indiarubber line-rimmed mouth
sags closed, you have to poke it with the fork
to make it open when you whisper "food".
Poke poke poke poke – tonight it's closed for keeps.'

The affair was at its height in *Cemetery*,
'She lies aslant a lettered slab unmoved,
stone Virgin newly down from the white plinth.
Because of Her, roots spring from graves cracked open
by Her descent. The love that makes bones live
moves even here warmed by her marble hand.'
Quite nice.

        But he could have his nasty side,
e.g. 'Misprint in Last Year's Horoscope'
(he was a Leo, me a Capricorn)
'That crap about a deep relationship
with, of all things, a Leo, was quite wrong.
It should have been: *avoid* Leos, they're losers,
they've no virility, they're bloody fairies,
they end up in the Arts or in the boozers.
You need a ram, a young ram, try an Aries.'

Or *Caricature Angel*, 'Christmas Eve,
I have strung up the Magi, Santa Claus,
Rudolph the Red-nosed Reindeer, Jesus Christ,
shepherds astonished, snowman with a pipe,
a perky robin. What I need most now
is a Madonna. Thumbing through the pile
of cards, I find a caricature angel
(signed, and with kisses now quite meaningless)
straddling in kinky boots an awed adorer.'

He seems not to have known I loved him then
(he married someone else) but found out later.

Widow

A perfectly round knot-hole
in the monumental mason's
fence reveals what might be
milk clotted in cold coffee
vortex of streaked grey veins.

The other side is polished
marble.

      A grave woman,
a diamond of black linen
sewn on the coat shoulder,
stoops, observes his progress.

Faint guide lines pre-ordain
the cold chisel.

           The mallet
knocks and a new shadow
sinks into deepening lines.

Absentees

Vinyl scoured of footmarks,
office a mausoleum,
typewriters muffled in hoods,
a clerk's ghost stirs in the cistern
and in the unoccupied cubicle,
the chain still swinging, the seat warm.

Broad Street hugely empty,
on each side deep-shadowed portals,
the wail of confident Methodists
from the red brick chapel is ended.

Only one single Volkswagen
still warm tick-ticks in contraction,
the owner so recently ghosted.

In a kiosk the earpiece still warm,
still-coiling smoke, the stubbed end
of another late occupier.

Absolute silence, absolute,
at my side a body's negative
in the appalling sheet.

Nocturne

Two concurrently are dreaming

I have got your	we have quarrelled
still warm ashes	and you leave me
in a plastic	without kissing
carrier bag	me goodbye but
fastened to my	three months later
palm with three inch	I ascend the
self-tap chrome screws	attic stairs to
which a former	find you brittle
lover tries to	unforgiven
free but can't turn	beard meshed tight with
anticlockwise	silver cobwebs

and wake up with night before them
each observing in the other's
pupil the familiar brightness
undimmed though a bloom reflects new
dark beyond the present bedroom.

Equinox

Daffodil ash speckles polished coffin wood.

Micrographs enlarge the dim region
beneath.

      Myxamoebae, plasmodia.
Eyeless stare back at me. *Chi se' tu,*
che vieni anzi ora?

          When it
was oak forest, charcoal-burners trod
this hollow. Even now, scrape away
one inch, their sour carbon lingers.

Limp overcoats of men, on a tree
are gibbeted, not one other living
soul stirs in all this black brake.

              We drain
away in the sod, warm March evening.
Buff doves black noosed rouse us with deep moans
hanging in Mortimer Tower.

              Our al fresco
is laced with acetic acid.

           I
descend a culling pit (unantlered
bucks' heads, stripped yellow pelts, entrails
in sealed plastic bags) and looking up see you
foreshortened.

         Smoke from a polished steel
Black Country crematorium chimney
enters me – sours smells of spring flowers on gravestones,
larch resin fragrant only from toothed steel.

Kwickie Service

Nobody else in the queue suspects
my world is not yours. You let fall
my cold hand, bloom smothers my eyes.

From the deserted stop you watch me.
I am now among the others.
My pennies rattle in the plastic bowl.
Doors whisper shut. This *Kwickie Service*
(I think I have never seen you so sad)
draws me towards the ferry to cross
from your side of the river to mine.

Us in The Ship

Estuary smell
of Bisque de Homard.

Us in The Ship

'why will you not
look in my eyes'

because I daren't.

We have become
close again now
after so long.

I must return
you must remain.

Moist saline lids.
Hands slipped from mine.

The dead channel.
The foetid swamp.
Eurydice.
An ancient sign
NEXT BOAT LEAVES AT...,
rotted away,
the hour is gone.

Mycologia

Edge of the brake

severed pink
cock of a dog
oozing goo
Mutinus caninus

foetid cream
old man's prick
in slimy erection
sucked by slugs
Phallus impudicus

striking deeper
the white white flesh
Amanita virosa
Destroying Angel

Trio

Alcohol,
night attire.

What is her
nightie like?
What sort of
underclothes?

He used to
recommend
books for me.
That was ten
years ago.
Each night he
reads to her;
I'd like that.

In her eyes
almost love
ten years since
ankle deep
acer leaves
and lime hearts
sapless, crushed.

Whispers he
loves me, but
what makes him
love her still?

Whispered he
loved me still,
OK why
marry her?

Would she still
willingly
love me now?

Would she be,
has she been,
willingly
screwed by him?

Do they think
I'd still be
willingly
loved by him?

On last year's
Christmas card
I, restrained,
wrote are you
happy/well?

Her letters'
reticence –
does she think
he does not
want me to
know she writes?

On last year's
Christmas card
I, restrained,
answered no
I'm not/not.

Extension
three three three

He may be
even now
ringing her.

I'm in town
for a week.

I shall be
occupied
each night till
half past nine
(that's the time
my, you know,
has to get
back to his
wife and kids)
sorry I

That's all right
quite OK
can't be helped
never mind.

How about
Saturday?

lovely. Look
forward to
seeing you.

Lovely. CLICK.

8 a.m.
Saturday
he leaves his
hotel room,
baths, Vosene
egg protein
hair shampoos,
by the glass
squeezes spots,
checks his tie
and departs.

One hundred
miles away
she's alone,
sleeps. Upstairs
hangs a drawn
pencil corpse
portrait of
him who now
distantly
checks his tie
and departs.

She awakes
does her face,
greens her eyes,
pouts, descends,
Maxwell House,
Radio 2.

Ferry, bus,
he descends.
Buys from a
florist mixed
daffodils/
irises.

10 a.m.
Weetabix.
He's away
for a week
she tells her
coffee cup.

Buys avo-
cado pears,
Brie, courgettes,
Burgundy,
chicken from
Sainsbury's.

He reads the
doors aloud
61
63
65
next one's hers
69.

He's away
for a week
she tells the
unmade bed.

12, she is
Hoovering,
door bell rings.

One thing I
never liked
was her hair.

Is the Brie
over-ripe?
Is the Beaune
good enough?

Will he make
rude remarks –
we had an
argument
once, about
wall to wall
carpeting.

One dozen
irises
one dozen
daffodils.

He'll be now
at her door.

What sort of
house is it?
What sort of
furniture?
What sort of
kitchen and
bathroom and
bedroom suite?

By the way,
Diana
sends her love.

All very
middle-class
all very
aimez-vous
Mon Repos?

Does she still
have long dark
lovely hair?

In your eyes
almost grief.
Tell me now.

He must have
been there now
several hours.

She could have
got him once
easily.

First there was
you who I
deeply loved
when too late.
Fill your glass.

Are they drunk?

Her marriage
soon went flat.

Then him I
married who
I thought I
loved enough.
Have some more?

If they get
drunk she may...

He said she's
hooked on a
married man,

Now when I
am in love
he is a
married man.

some people
court bad luck.
In vino
veritas
I'm afraid
for them both.

Funny how
things turn out.
Encore Beaune?

When Puss dies
I'll be lost.
Your eyes are
very blue.

Solo now
I sing flat:
youth must with
age decay
beauty will
fade away
castles are
sacked in war
chieftains are
scattered far

I'm afraid
to grow old.
I wouldn't
have TV
but for the
loneliness.
Why did you
marry her?

I loved her
very much,
and still do.
Not to say
that in my
loving her
I was not
deeply in
love with you,
and still am.

love is a
fixèd star
ha ha ha
ha ha ha.

He now leaves
69
takes her arm.

6 p.m.
she prepares
one boiled egg.

Takes his arm
at the door.

Bus arrives
he boards bus
drops fare in
plastic bowl
waves to her
watching him
from the stop,
bus departs.

slices toast
in thin strips

Bus station
6.30
she gazes
into his
eyes, he waves,
she waves back,
he from bus
she from stop,
bus departs

6.40
of the whole
two dozen
passengers
he looks most
lachrymose.

dips them in
absently.

she appears
sadder than
anyone
else in sight.

8 at night
Saturday.
Dines with friends,
too much Krug
with Hors-d'Oeuvres
too much Bual
with dessert.

VHF
Saturday
evening play:
TIME present
SCENE bedroom
sensual
whisperings
(modern stuff).

Hurls empties
into bin.
Sniffs vase of
flowers, smiles,
sits alone
with TV.

10 p.m.
Saturday
he phones up:
nosh wish to
trude introo
simly a
soshul call
no wish trude   What are they
no wish tall   doing now?
nottot tall
nottot at
losh love losh
love losh love.   She answers
                     telephone:
                     love you're drunk

                     goodnight love.

Past midnight.   Trusting his   Insular,
Unconscious.   love she sleeps –   wrapped in white
                  cellular   glacial sheets.
                  warmth of bed.

                  How was she?   What have I
                                      done? Why me?
                                      (Love me, love
                                      my black cat.)

                                      I loved him
                                      but too late
                                      (love me, love
                                      my black cat).

                                      My husband
                                      I disliked
                                      (love me, love
                                      my black cat).

                                      I love a
                                      married man
                                      (love me, love
                                      my black cat).

Can't things go
right just once?
(Love me, love
my black cat.)

Now in the
women's ward
uterus
near defunct
(love me, love
my black cat).

Seemed OK

Otto Van Bumph

Mr Bottomly taught us French and Eng. Lit.
We called him Otto Van Bumph, I don't know why now.
When we were in 4D he was absent
nearly a whole term. When he returned
he got tired climbing the stairs and short of breath.
We took the piss with a rare tenderness.
One day at his desk he rested his head
in his hands and panted gently, his face
went battleship-grey. To move from one's seat
was punishable by lines but Frank Martin
walked straight up to him, put his hand on his arm
and said 'Sir, do you want a glass of water?'

Was there a bereaved Frau Van Bumph? I don't know.
But the Headmaster, Bunny Warren, displayed
a convincingly tremulous voice when he made
the announcement. Of course there was a whip-round.
And an eighth-rate print of *The Young Mozart*
hung outside the Assembly Hall
testifies to his having been *sort of* loved
by, among others, Craigy, Rodge Sowerby,
Al Willis, Phil Horton and me.

Mem-sahib

'Such a pity he was the way he was,
because he was such a clever man –
he could speak five languages including
Urdu and what they talk in the Punjab.
Calcutta was such an exciting place,
I was sorry to leave – of course I told him
I was just going to visit Mother.
Those two months on a cargo-vessel
were bliss – to be sailing away from him!
But he was, oh, such a handsome man,
somehow he seemed to make all occasions
special, out of the ordinary.
But every rupee he had went on drink –
I had to sell my few special things, jewels,
a locket Mother had sent me and so on,
to buy little things for myself you know.
When he was drunk and he always was drunk
he was horrid, horrid – he'd cause such scenes
and absolutely humiliate one
in public places, restaurants and so on.
He came to Mother's afterwards begging,
begging me to go back to him – never!
Mother kept saying "I told you so. I
told you he was a low type." I never
ate their horrid curries, he never ate
anything else and whisky, whisky –
probably he got ulcers years ago,
I hope he did and he's dead dead DEAD now.'

Correspondence

Dear Martin,
              Bumped into Arthur tonight
(after a concert of, can you guess?
Sibelius – do you remember how
you and I loved his 2nd and 7th?)
and we got talking somehow about you.
I'm back here now. I had to write to you.
My marriage turned out a bit of a mess.
How are you? Drop me a line,
                     Love,
                        Heather.

Dear Heather,
              Just a note to thank you for
writing. My marriage has broken up. Karen
has gone to live in a caravan with
a Welsh self-taught painter who recently
got a grant from the Welsh Arts Council to make
a cartoon film. She took the child with her.
I'm living here at the house and would like
to see you if you could make it,
                     Love,
                        Martin.

Dear Clive,
              Just a few lines to tell you the
score. My marriage has broken up. Karen
has gone to live in a caravan with
a Welsh self-taught painter who recently
got a grant from the Welsh Arts Council to make
a cartoon film. She took the child with her.
I'm living here at the house with a girl
called Heather,
              Hope to see you soon,
                        Mart.

Dear Clive,

I came across Arthur the other
night. (I'd been to a concert of Symphonies
2 and 7 by Sibelius –
thought of those 78s you bought me!)
Somehow we started talking about you.
Marriage for Martin and me was a mess.
I went to live with an artist – but now...well,
never mind. Drop me a line,

Love,

Karen.

Dear Karen,

I'm on my own again now.
Me and Heather have parted company.
I feel sorry about it – lonely
and sad would be more accurate. But
I couldn't live with her any more
I'm afraid. I feel I've sort of betrayed her –
and now I think I prefer being hurt to
hurting someone else,

All the best,

Martin.

Dear Karen,

Just a short note to say thanks for
writing. I'd heard from Mart that you'd broken up.
Sorry to hear it – you know I was always
very very fond of you. I should've
liked to invite you over some time but, well,
it's a bit awkward to tell you the truth, I'm
sort of involved with someone called Heather – look,
why not come over and see us *both*?

Love,

Clive.

Luncheon

I was on my way to Broadcasting House
to make a recording for George MacBeth's
programme *Poetry Now* of a poem
incorporating a desperate phone
conversation with a young woman whom
I had been much in love with years before,
and having two hours to spare decided
to lunch at a Restaurant in Charlotte Street.

I sat in a leather upholstered chair
in Reception, drank a large Campari
with two ice chunks and a whoosh of soda,
then ate plump olives and crisp hot radish
perusing the menu and wine list. I
had just crunched my third pink radish and was
intent on a fat sleek black olive (bloomed
with a surface film of oil sufficient
to make fingerprints when I picked it up)
when close to my ear a telephone bell
rang from an alcove across which was drawn
a drape of red and gold Regency stripes.
I quite liked the look of the '66
Chambertin and, intending to order
roast beef and half a bottle, I motioned
the waiter, a Mediterranean type,
but he went straight past me behind the drape.
A long pause 'Margaret, donta speak mad'.
I thought I might start with cold Vichyssoise
'for Godasake Margaret coma roun queek'
he reappeared '(donna mia) yes sir
you lika to placa de order now, si,
de rostabif good'. Ice-cold Vichyssoise,
then a thing like a huge tureen on wheels
with spirit-lamps under it was brought in,
the lid was thrown open revealing steam
sputtering out in gushes from shoulder
and flank of a quarter of English beef.
One in a red blazer struck steel and carved
thick foolscap slices of lean meat roasted

charcoal-crisp at the outside, a bead
of blood welling at the raw centre. Then
the telephone bell again 'greena beans,
scusa please, nota keep one moment' I
helped myself to greens. The Burgundy
turned out excellent full and fruity with
bottle-age starting to show – the colour
reddy-brown at the meniscus, the tannin
present but mellowed not shrivelling the palate
'for Godasake Margaret leesten please'.
Strawberries fresh-bought from Covent Garden
dunked in Marsala drenched in double cream.
Only fifteen minutes had gone since
the telephone last rang, but during dessert
it went again. The waiter answered
'I tolda you Margaret coma roun queek
you mus be crazy don say doza theengs'.
I had to insist on Kenya coffee –
I find it much lighter after a meal –
with which I had one large V.S.O.P.
then asked the waiter to get a taxi
which reached the door ten minutes later
just as the telephone started to ring.

Discarded Note

Dear Pete,
             (to whom she did not ever post this
discarded note) *I'm writing from the ward.*
Last time we met we talked about our two
separate lives, how each of us preferred
to have avoided aimless procreation,
not merely bred. Appeasing to be childless,
to live and die unique, to end the line,
have no connection with the bloody mess
to come. And pharmaceutics obviate
the need for kids, if Minovlar should fail
syringe it out and squirt it down the bogs.

All very well, but now I'm faced with this
irrevocable uterotomy
even in me the bestial part wins,
'unable to have babies' leaves me a stunned
primeval female craving pregnancy –
the outmoded evolutionary urge,
to which you are immune being a male
and biologically unsympathetic
to mere irrational femininity.

Prolonged Look

Prolonged look sneaked at you after so long;
profile I nearly married you for still lovely,
but, green smeared from your eyes, face cleansed for bed,
your last few years' bad times show as bags of putty,
you're getting just a wee bit puggy my love.

> Hir bowgy cheekes been as softe as clay,
> With large jowes and substancial.
> Thus Thomas Hoccleve of his grotesque lady.

> Christ when I sid er, sorry an again!
> I knowed it's er I topped an tailed years since,
> thank Christ us never wed – look on er now!
> Drunk echoes from the overcrowded Globe.

Not funny. You grow actually ugly
and my still loving you makes it no better.

Ballad

I'll tell you all a story
   concerning John and Joan;
in student days each clung to each
   as flesh will cling to bone,

as a fluke clings to a liver or
   a lichen to a stone
Joan would cling to Jonathan
   Jonathan to Joan,

as Eurydice and Orpheus
   as Leda and the Swan
as Hero and Leander
   so were Joan and John.

You would see them at a lecture
   on *Les Fauves* or *Les Nabis*
or *Intimisme*, sat at the back,
   his hand above her knee.

You would see him at a seminar
   discussing Form or Taste
or Aesthetics or Cybernetics
   with his arm round her waist.

You would see her in a life class
   cross-hatching aimlessly
gawping at not the model but
   John and his charcoal 6B.

You would hear them talk through lunchtime
   (of Puvis de Chavannes,
Erich Heckel, Karl Schmidt-Rottluff,
   Maurice Denis, Mondrian,

Matthew Smith, Odilon Redon,
   Edvard Munch, Chaim Soutine,
Emil Nolde) holding hands
   in the college canteen.

John had a one-room basement flat
  in Percy Street, where she
would dust or satisfy his lust
  (to a certain degree)

or tidy up or make a cup
  of lotus blossom tea
or iron or sew, but was prompt to go
  at midnight (usually).

And he would walk her to the stop
  to board the late night bus
and he'd kiss her glove then see his love
  borne to the terminus.

Now they would have liked to marry,
  or at least co-reside,
but the Calvinist prigs where she was in digs—
  aunts on her mother's side –

forbade her staying out all night,
  disliked him from the start,
said 'anything might happen at that
  permissive College of Art'.

You could see them growing separate
  yet could not interfere.
They were doing Dip. A.D.,
  their penultimate year.

You could see them quarrel more and more
  with each successive week.
In their final year of A.T.D.
  things had reached a peak.

One day John said to Joan 'Joan
  you're becoming a bore'.
Joan said to John 'John I don't want
  to go with you any more'.

And so they finished there and then.
　　It's cliché but it's sound –
what they say about no good coming
　　of love on the rebound.

For John got stuck, it was just his luck,
　　(to cut a long story short)
with a girl he'd filled at a party
　　who you'd never have thought

could fit Joan's niche, but he married the bitch,
　　bought a place, settled down,
got a teaching job at a Secondary Mod.
　　in the roughest end of town.

And Joan got wed to a bloke who was Head
　　of Games at a school where she
found herself a post teaching Art to a host
　　of snotty-nosed peasantry.

　　　　*　　*　　*　　*

On a spring day ten years later
　　a small assembly
of teachers met to discuss and set
　　papers for CSE

and one of those teachers was John
　　who now had a Scale 4 post
and the next to come in was Joan, drawn and thin,
　　and you'd think she'd seen a ghost

the way she blanched when she saw him,
　　said 'John, I didn't think...'
He said 'thank Christ I've seen you – let's slip off
　　for a talk and a drink'.

In the snug of The Grapes she told him,
　　through whisky laced with tears,
her marriage was bad and her husband hadn't
　　slept with her for two years.

And John said, sucking his Guinness head
    creamily off the top,
'between me and you my marriage is through,
    it's been an almighty flop'.

And Joan said, watching the barmaid
    draw another pint of stout,
'it's funny ha ha ha ha ha ha
    funny how things turn out'.

The Prison Cell & Barrel Mystery

Asked to set the table

incongruously I find myself
suddenly in the chilled garden at dusk
distracted perhaps by two I passed earlier
pressed close extracting more than usual
savour from kissing – the line of the girl's
cheek so reproduced yours that personae
and time shifted.

        Your brittle account of
marriage to someone else as 'a bit
of a mess' rustles now again from tremulous
leaves.

    I am outside.

        Through glass the warm hearth.

Fleetingly trodden thyme shrouds me bruised
irredeemably under my own weight.

       *

In a glass catafalque he
eyes the black receiver, lips
set, soundproofed fingers drum
the double beat and pause of
a ringing call unanswered

one minute elapses

a young woman approaches,
suddenly recognises
him within, audibly
inhales, taps the glass twice

'you're just the same' indicates
they have not met for some time,

as if resurrected
he emerges, hands join
familiar as old
well made dovetails.

*

Anthracite seams prise open, gush.
You re-kindle your flat fire.
Panes bloom, admit only dark now.

Remember from under ground
(wormwood, Shadows, The Stones)
ascending into a city
drenched in sun, embracing?

You whisper what I have not known
until now – only reticence
caused you to turn away then.

Sealed for these aeons in dark
vegetal pressure, a breath bursts,
ignites, unshadows your temple.

*

I have worn this jacket a decade; its first
night out you deposited a dark copper
hair on the shoulder which I kept
in a page of *La Vita Nuova* where
it still is. Tonight you implant another
mysteriously under the heart where
a week from now I am to discover it
scarcely less lustrous than at first.

*

Awaking to your
holding my head
and a glass to my lips
I thought a system of
converse ironies
in operation
and we after all
were together.

        The cold
that struck my bowels then
was at her absence –
changing to grief at
recalling how fleeting
is this our reunion.

I have not seen you
for so long now that
you count as a corpse.

Already you dress
put black on your eyes
to cross the river
again for the city.

        *

Your number is being rung
I request your extension

shall we meet again tonight
I return tomorrow

I shall wait anyway
meet me there if you possibly can

meet me there if you possibly can
meet me there if you poss

the line's down speak up
I am crossed with a man in the corn trade

buying Number Three Corn
ex the S.S. *Arrivederci.*

*

The Post House almost unchanged – our table
occupies the same place on the stairs,
mahogany Bacchus impartially
glares from a cluster of maturer vintage,

The Change Up and The Change Down are not
evident now, but a pleasant vignette
of what the old place was is rooted
still in these walls, a Music Hall playbill
revives THE OLD SPECTACULAR,

                                       regulars
seem the same though most might tell you
of ten years' ironies almost to match
our own.

            Gone ten...

                        you won't make it now...

'licensed hours is licensed hours sir!'...

again tonight after ten years, unchanged,
we still pursue separate double ironies...

ghosts of THE GREATEST SHOW IN THE WORLD,
THE WINNERS OF THE GREAT HANDCUFFS CONTEST,
THE PRISON CELL & BARREL MYSTERY.

A · Mon · Sevl · Desir

I used to re-read your letters for hours
hoping to decode some amative message
I'd missed first time – I'd even peer into
the envelope to see if you'd written
your declaration of love for me there;
you never had.

                  Today I read into
'La Dame à la Licorne', this Greetings Card
you send me, more than you mean – erect horn,
sumptuous tent, invitingly velvet and
silk aloof Lady poised at the entrance drapes,
and, above all, A · MON · SEVL · DESIR.

OK I read too much into them, but
you do write nice things to me now, at last.
When we could have done something about it
our affection was inarticulate –
now, a dozen years late, all we *can* do is
write affectionate things to each other.

Thanksgiving

Perhaps I could have expected
to discover you, my wife's sister,
attractive, pleasant to be with,
but you took me by surprise
(well, I hadn't seen you for years)
and rescued me after dinner
when the rest were boring, BORING,
and the Late-Bottled Port gone.

My thanks to your sister who
patiently suffered their fool
conversation, didn't despise me
for being even more than
usually rude and outrageous,
gave us the OK to sneak off.

And my thanks to you Christine love
who never caused me to yawn once
in our stolen couple of hours
at the comfy Rose & Crown
but neatly dissected their claptrap,
laughed, warmed to Wilfred Owen,
spoke of the boy in love with you,
Life's Little Ironies,
patiently suffered my sotted
No-God and Species Decline stuff,

and charmed me, Christine, entirely.

Near-Miss

Spring in Myrtle Street on the fire-escape
she said NO and I felt a fool. But we
grew closer over the years, fell in love
each with the other quite genuinely –
but not, regrettably, concurrently.

Duologues

1

'Whabout that piece as lives on the farm
you delivers to, Stokey? Er as you fancies?
Up-over somewheres, Furrow Ill is it? Or
Mount Flirt or Stonewall Ill or The Warren?'

                                          'Oh,
you means er out Boultibrooke way. I
knowed er long afore ever I come
to drive for South Shropshire Farmers. Well,
er inna bad lookin mind, just one thing –
they reckons as ers a bit loony like. See,
er bloke (im as ad that motor bike crack
comin ome off the piss that time Gonder's Neck way)
e got buried in Boultibrooke churchyard
as lies at back of the farmuss, so
as er looks out er bedroom er sees is stone and
they reckons as ow er throws fits and falls
in a ruck evertime er thinks on it.'

2

'That piece as Vaughany were toppin an tailin,
us inna sid er for a bit – er as served
at the King's Arms.'

                              'Ers jed a cancer, mon, died,
oh, months since. Er was in Ludlow ospital
weeks – course old Vaughany couldna go visit er,
account of er usband were allus there, so
e rings up Matron everday, asks
ow er is. Course old Matron wants to know
oo e is – e says as ees makin enquiries
for a friend of ers in Ereford. Well,
when Matron tells er as an Ereford friend
sends love to er, er knowed well enough then
it was Vaughany – see they'd arranged it previous.

After a bit mind, er old brain gets fuddled like
(er went stiff a day or two after) and
er says to Matron "what friend in Ereford?"
So nex time e rings, Matron asks old Vaughany
"what's the name of this Ereford friend?" Well,
never a flicker mind, Vaughany says "Alice
as works in Woolworths in Ereford." Thats
the last as ever e ad to do with er.'

3

'I wish I'd knowed im as drives tractor, afore I wed Jim.
Once you marries the wrong un youm never the same someow.'

'Same along o me, Annie, that un as I fancied first,
e never said much all them years as us was courtin,
so I thinks as e dunna like me, an breaks up with im.
Then e thinks as I dunna like im, an takes some wench else.
Then I sid im again, one Pig Day it were in the Arms,
and e says as e loves me an would I get wed to im
(only would I answer im quick or eed af to wed er).
Well, I never says "ar" nor "no" for days, till e thinks
as it's "no" and e weds this other out Clungunford way
an they moves down Tenbury country – Glebe Farm an summat.
An e dunna get on with er, an just now e writes me
as e loves me, an I writes back as I loves im an all.
Just now all is stock dies – that Foot and Mouth year afore last –
and they says as e got debts an that's why e shot isself.'

Soirée

One funny thing about loving someone
is how much you'll put up with – her parents'
conversazione for example,
or being sweet to these fools she works with
who smoke inferior cigars and think
it's savoir vivre, and drag me back to drink
inadequately and long past my bedtime,
and put on records (God!) stuff like Ray Conniff.
And all their damn fool questions 'tell me Peter,
what do you write *about*?' (cunts like you, mate).
'Peter, you interested in history?'
(Mate, I ain't even interested in
the present.) Still I'm here because I love her.

Ménage à Trois

'Make yourself coffee, and *feel* the place.'
Said the psychologist's mistress and the
psychologist's wife and the psychologist
to Michael when he arrived.

                                So he sat
in the kitchen drinking black Nescafé
while in the garden the psychologist's
mistress lay on the lawn and pretended
to read Gide from a grubby thumbed Penguin.
Over Michael in the kitchen clambered
nude and T-shirted malicious infants
(sired by the psychologist, of both his wife
and his mistress) with chocolate and phlegm
besmirching their jowls in equal amounts.

High Summer. He heard through the open door
a buzzard mew on an aloof thermal.

In the Ballroom music was playing. The
psychologist and his wife were dancing.
Strauss wafted through the open French window.

Suddenly the psychologist's mistress
leapt from the lawn, let out a loony yell,
'A*A*A*A*A*A*A*A*AGH!
WHY MUST HE TAUNT ME TAUNT ME TAUNT ME SO?!',
ran upstairs, Strauss stopped on the gramophone.
All the kiddies snivelled orchestrally.

Upstairs bounded the psychologist,
rowed with his doxy, rushed down, said 'damn, DAMN!',
jumped on a little Japanese motor bike,
revved up and roared off – brrrm brrrm brrrm brrrm.

Wife and mistress shrieked, scratched, screeched, bit, tore, spat.
Michael shouted 'you are all mad, mad, MAD!',
ran to his Renault, got in, started up,
when out rushed the wife and the mistress of
the psychologist (Michael locked his door)
and snarled through the windscreen wagging their fingers
'we may be mad, Michael, but, GOD, IT'S REAL.'

Gravel drive crunched, he accelerated.
Outside the gate he thought 'I must remember
this for my novel. Meanwhile I must tell
my friend Peter Reading about it – he'll
probably find it terribly funny.'

NOTHING FOR ANYONE

(1977)

*(Mercifully, we're only
molested by the Big Issue
in the watches of the night:
in daylight hours we busy
ourselves with the Trivial)*

Hymn

We're crusted enough to know
we can't immortalise this,
but gooey enough to want to
try to honour a morning
as honeyed as England ever
gifted a couple of spooners with.

So let's hymn this: that at 8
on a summer morning the dew,
licked from the roses we nuzzle
nose to nose in the garden
of lichened Pipe Aston Church,
is luscious as Gewürztraminer.

And if anyone wants to see
they can in the Visitors' Book
our puny dignified gesture
(the most we can do, Little Mortal,)
that today we are here. 17th
of June 1975.

Sonnet

Nine years of formal marriage (not to mention
the practice-run at College), to be candid,
are not devoid of some domestic tension –
'Why can't you do bread sauce with cloves, like Gran did?',
'Who left the frigging bedroom light on all day?',
or, the real nitty-gritty, 'I regret
having had you back when you'd had it away
with that bitch!' – as in most ménages. And yet,
in nine years, they have got acclimatised
to privacies too blushful to admit
even to close friends (who'd be scandalised
by, for example, their bad taste in Lit. –
like actually *reading* H.G. Wells);
in short, neither could *stand* anyone else.

' "Iuppiter ex alto periuria ridet amantum" 15s 6d'

A lady's album of 1826
in my possession, contains the following.

***   ***   ***

Two songs – 'Dear Maid, I Love Thee (andantino)',
'Why Hast Thou Taught Me To Love Thee? (allegro)'.

***   ***   ***

'Dear Helen, on my life, I vow,
And 'tis a sacred token,
The friendship which unites us now,
By me, shall ne'er be broken.

(R.S. September 1826.)'

***   ***   ***

'Extempore Lines Addressed To Helen

If to esteem thee be a crime,
I ne'er can be forgiven;
If doomed to love thee and repine, –
Be merciful, kind heaven.

(E.H. Nov. 1826 Leeds.)'

***   ***   ***

'Should pleasure be my future lot,
Or human cares o'ertake me,
This pledge shall never be forgot,
This heart shall not forsake thee.

(R.S. Brighton. May 1827)'

***   ***   ***

'CONTEMPLATION (FOR A LADY'S ALBUM)', written by
E.H. in July 1827 in Hastings, is illegible apart from two
underlined fragments:

'... my desolate heart...'

'... in our first, happier days...'

***   ***   ***

'EPITHALAMIUM (FOR MY BRIDE, HELEN) by E.H.
Jan. 1828, London.' is wholly illegible.

***   ***   ***

A contribution entitled 'Early Love – lines addressed
to a young lady from her mother' is badly foxed, and
illegible apart from the opening paragraph:

'Nothing is perhaps more dangerous to the
future happiness of women of our thoughts
and cultured habits, than the entertaining
of an early, long, and unfortunate attach-
ment...'

***   ***   ***

More songs:

'The Bride's Farewell',
'To A Faded Flower',
'Oh! No, We Never Mention Him'.

***   ***   ***

Illegible; then:

'With ardent flame and honest heart
I'll never cease to love thee!

RS. (London, March 1828)'

***   ***   ***

'A boat at midnight sent alone
To drift upon the moonlit sea;
A wounded bird, who has but one
Imperfect wing...' (illegible) '...
Is like what I am without thee!

R.S. (Edinburgh, Jun. 1829)'

***   ***   ***

'Once more, enchanting girl, adieu!
I must be gone while yet I may.
Oft shall I weep to think of you,
But here I will not, cannot stay!

O could I – No! It must not be!
Adieu! A long, a long adieu!
– Yet still, methinks, you frown on me,
Or never could I fly from you!

(R.S., site of John Groot's House, Dec. 1829)'

***   ***   ***

'NEWINGTON BOOKSHOP
LIVERPOOL
1962'

on the endpaper. And in a cryptic academic hand:
' "Iuppiter ex alto periuria ridet amantum" 15s 6d.'

Diptych

'Do you remember
at College of Art
in a Seminar once
when all of us were
discussing reasons
why we all painted,
and all decided
our motivation
was Communication?
Then that little bloke
(what was his name? He
seemed always half-cut,
Reading or something)
suddenly said
"Well *I* don't paint
to communicate.
In fact the reverse –
to alienate;
to paint out the clues
any audience
might otherwise get." '

'Met Di Reading's husband
so naturally asked
"How's the old Poetry?"
He didn't respond –
damned unsociable.
Stuck with him, I said
"Your wife once read me
one of your poems –
are you approaching
a wider audience
by being witty?"
But all he said was
"My books are only
an ego-boosting
filing system.
If no one buys them
I'll be sad because
Secker & Warburg
will not love me and
manuscript pages
don't look so good." '

On Hearing the First Cuckoo in Spring

Unbearable: (1) listening
to music any more (unless
in the safe company of others),
(2) vegetal spring stirrings –

each an insufferable glimpse,
a split-second's primal clarity,
of Not-Quite-Graspable Potential/
Dimly-Recollected Guilt.

The John o' Groat's Theory

'When Alison left Gregory for Miles
Gregory went to pieces. Angela –
that's Miles's wife – was not resentful, but
she went to pieces also. As for Mark –
that's Alison and Greg's elder boy – he
got a complex and started throwing knives.
Russell – their younger – got a nervous lisp.
Sally and Abigail – Angela's girls
by her first marriage – urinate in class
(their Headmaster says this is natural).
Penny and Gordon – Miles and Angela's
own children – are quite normal, but *will* ask
"When is our Daddy coming home again?"
Mr and Mrs Smythe – Miles's parents –
were terribly upset; they'd always said
"Miles and his wife are *so* compatible."
Angela's people took it even worse;
her mother – Esther Everoyd – has been
prostrate since hearing of it. (Mr E.
is Angela's stepfather, actually.
Her father is a Mr Inkerman
who visits her still – Angela, that is –
but doesn't seem to care that they're divorced.)
The Atwells, who are Gregory's parents,
have all their work cut out trying to care
for Gregory – he's hospitalised now.
Mr and Mrs Hotchkinson, you know –
Alison's parents – seem embarrassed more
than upset (I've a feeling they were pleased
when Alison left Gregory for Miles).'

                              *

'well I'm broad-minded, *but*'

                              'a bloody lout –
pardon my French'

'he *really* was *too* much'

'no way to treat a wife'

                    'well I've heard "language",
what with the Rugby Club and all that, *but*,
well, he was going just a bit *too* far'

'he said to Howard "You can 'eff off', too" –
in front of *women*'

                    'well I'm broad-minded, *but*'

*

'There are two letters – one from my sister and one from Mummy.
I'll read them out to you "Dear Sue, How do you like my super
new writing paper? At least it doesn't weigh very much. I'm at
Mum's this weekend as it's Jenny's last weekend. She spent all
morning packing and left at 12.30 with Andrea and her father in
their car. Richard has been staying here this weekend as well. We
all had a good time at Christmas except that Mummy caught my
bug I think and wasn't feeling too good on Boxing Day. Roger
came up for New Year and we all stayed here on Thursday and
Friday. We played a lot of games including 'Formula 1' which
Jenny and Richard bought me. We went to my flat on the Friday
night as we had to try out my new casserole dish. We made a super
meal with steak and kidney, swede, onion, carrots and dumplings
and we had a bottle of wine as well. Roger brought all his stereo
equipment with him so we listened to a lot of records and played
'Formula 1'. It was the weekend of the wind so I was glad Roger
was there as he is a tower of strength. Some of the houses lost
tiles and fences but mine was OK. Thank you very much for the
tea-cosy and stand. Both just what I needed of course. Now my
second cup of tea isn't cold and up till now I'd been using the
whole tea-tray as a stand (also that cutting board you gave me).
Pity about leaving all your presents in the Left Luggage Office,
still, it sounds as if you enjoyed your return journey. I suppose
you're back now at work. I must say I envy you your long holi-
days. Next week is Roger's Works Dinner-Dance so am looking
forward to it except I'm so overweight I haven't got anything to

wear. The following week is our Managers' Dinner so I don't think I'm going to lose much weight in the next fortnight. My New Year's Resolution is to lose 1½ stone before my birthday. Jenny was over 10 stone this morning so if I could lose that much I'd be lighter than her! Mummy and Daddy are in the garden cutting down trees and broken branches. One went last night outside the lounge front window. A whole tree went over at the top of the road the previous weekend pulling up a gas main. The lights were also out here for about 2 hours. We had blood collectors at work the other day so decided to go just to see what blood group I am. I remember you going when you were at Art College. Anyway the last thing I said was 'You can't faint lying down.' I now know that you can! It really was quite funny in that I didn't feel as if I was going to at all. I just did and I came back not knowing where I was. I think that's about it. Hope you didn't catch my bug when you were here. Happy New Year. Love from Debbie. P.S. Glad to hear Donald is back from his 'holiday' and hope all goes well for you both again and works this time." And the other one says "Dear Susan, Very many thanks for lovely Christmas presents. We have already enjoyed the Arthur Negus Antiques book and have found much to interest us. So far we have not sampled the crystallised fruits, but I know we will enjoy that luxury soon. Debbie has given you most of the news, I'll just add a few lines. Jenny phoned to say she had settled into the university life again, and the trip by car was OK. On Friday evening we had a phone call from David, he was in London on his return flight to USA. He had been on a business trip to the Philips plant in Holland and expects to make the trip every three months. Of course being a top man in computers means his firm looks after him very well, it is a very well paid job and very very secure. It's such a nice morning here (Tuesday) Dad and I are about to start moving soil in preparation for the new greenhouse. Daddy mowed the lawn yesterday – a little bit early in the year, I think, but it now looks very smart and it now remains for me to finish the edges. Hope you are right in taking D back like that, without a murmur – still, you know best of course. Expect you have now settled back to work routine again. Hope all goes well. Lots and lots of love, Mummy." Don't tell me you haven't been listening darling, I said "There are two letters – one from my sister and one from Mummy. I'll read them out to you 'Dear Sue, How do you like my super new writing paper?...' " '

*

'Shh! I want to hear this bloke on the box.'

'... that however close to someone you are,
however perfect and irreplaceable
seems the union, in reality
transplant yourself twenty years back anywhere –
John o' Groat's, say – and benign Biology
will lead you to love someone else and believe
you love them exclusively, so uniquely
it couldn't have happened with anyone else
anywhere else. Which is to say
we are most of us perfectly capable
of falling in love (to a fairly profound
degree) with any or all of a larger
cross-section of the opposite sex
than normal social and matrimonial
codes make it comfy to realise...'

'E.g. I have fallen in love with you
without falling out of love with my wife.'

Almanac

Byron was born in January
(Good Art mitigates bad conduct).

A hyacinth bursts its pot
and stirs in the darkened cupboard.

Narcissus pseudonarcissus,
Viola odorata and
Primula vulgaris, WELCOME!

All Fools' Day. Inland Revenue
and Church start their year on the 5th.

Twits with bells on their ankles
belt each other with pig bladders.

Even regarding the rose
through world-coloured spectacles,
the worldliest yawner is still awed.

July 27th, my birthday.
It worries me more being thirty
than not being nice to know.

Bank Holiday. Oafs at Blackpool,
remember, are the same species
as, say, Catullus or Eliot.

In the 'Arms, glum farmers inform us
that their Peniarth oats are down
(no tears, though, dilute their doubles).

October, coloured by dying.

On my personal bonfire this year:
singers of rugby songs, Yogaists,
schoolteachers and Health Food freaks.

Secular (thus hopeless) hangovers –
dead tree, surfeit of calories,
cards bought for Spastics, nuts.

Response

'...The idea is to write a poem about,
or in some way deriving from, Shakespeare,
a play, a character, a quotation – something
of that kind. Would you be interested in this?'

Dear Brownjohn,

           Since you wrote me on behalf
of the World Centre for Shakespeare Studies and asked
if I'd be interested in contributing
to 'Poems for Shakespeare' (and I said O.K.)
I have had nine nights of recurrent nightmare
wherein I balls up Act 1 Scene 2 thus:

    '...Caesar said to me, "Dar'st thou, Cassius, now
    Leap in with me into this angry flood,
    And swim to yonder point?" Upon the word,
    Accoutred as I was, I plungèd in,
    And bade him follow: so, indeed, he did.
    The torrent roar'd; and we did buffet it
    With lusty sinews, throwing it aside,
    And stemming it with hearts of controversy:
    But ere we could arrive the point propos'd,
    Caesar cried, "Dar'st thou, Cassius, now
    Leap in with me into this angry flood,
    And swim to yonder point?" Upon the word,
    Accoutred as I was, I plungèd in,
    And bade him follow: so, indeed, he did.
    The torrent roar'd; and we did buffet it
    With lusty sinews, throwing it aside,
    And stemming it with hearts of controversy:
    But ere we could arrive the point propos'd,
    Caesar cried, "Dar'st thou, Cassius, now
    Leap in with me into this angry flood,
    And swim to yonder point?" Upon the word,
    Accoutred as I was, I plungèd in,
    And bade him follow: so, indeed, he did.
    The torrent roar'd; and we did buffet it
    With lusty sinews, throwing it aside,
    And stemming it with hearts of controversy:

But ere we could arrive the point propos'd,
Caesar cried, "Dar'st thou, Cassius, now" '

I am imprisoned centrifugally
the Globe spins and the Gods are hissing 'OFF!'
those in the cheap seats who're not bored are angry
the trapdoor in the planks suddenly yawns
Caesar cries 'Help me, Cassius, or I sink!'
I am with dust and other discarded props
beneath the stage where real depth is cardboard
the Capitol is brittle polystyrene
my heart is in the coffin there with Caesar
I lick ash from the sockets of dry skull
this is not how I had envisaged it

– nor, I imagine, what you had in mind.
I think perhaps you'd better count me out.

Placed by the Gideons

The top stair creaks. At the end of the landing
the carpet changes to faded flesh.
An exponent of the compliant smirk
welcomed me, carried my case for pence.
Plywood firedoors snap shut.

A warped latch forced (yellow *Times* lines the wardrobe)
rattles bone shoulders to hang your coat on.
YOU MAY DRIP-DRY IN THE WASTEPAPER BIN.
A varnished oblong, ruled-round with dust, is
left by the Book.

Where to find help when assailed by...Doubt...Debt...
Death – John 11. 25, 26.
...the resurrection and...though he were dead...
and believeth in me, shall never die.
Believeth thou this?

Post-Dated

I trust they are not yet too close for comfort,
you still turn, I presume, Mother and Father,
on rare occasions when you see the *Echo*,
to those hilarious In Memoriams
(funnier, even, than the Closing Prices) –
'God wanted him a Heavenly harp to play,
And so He took our dear old Dad away!',
'We loved you since you pushed us in the pram,
But Holy Jesus took you! Dearest Mam.'

Don't worry; when your times come, you'll be spared
the claptrap.

        But perhaps you'd have preferred
not to have had the dubious distinction
of a post-dated epitaph. However:
THANK YOU FOR HAVING BEEN WHAT PARENTS SHOULD BE –
BENIGNER THAN THEIR WITLESS BROOD DESERVES.

Ah well, my Loves, have this and welcome *now* –
memorials are wasted on their victims.

Travelogue

It used to be a tiny place until –
a bunch of whizz-kid architects had done
their stuff. Ten dozen brash unfinished cheap
concrete and warped pine cantilevered lumps
of arty-farty blocks and knick-knack shops
await completion for the winter takings.

But now it's August and it's pissing down.
Construction gangs are rained-off, ski-lifts drip,
hotels are all FERMETURE ANNUELLE,
La Place de Jeunesse is portcullised shut,
dust rests on skiing tanned shop-window dummies,
board pavements echo, you can't get a drink.

A child spoons from a damp pile left by builders
grey wet grit on the head of his drenched puppy.
Marooned, a stone-built shack (hens on dirt floor)
and a bewildered oldie – the only one
dourly expecting not to show a profit
after this winter's sport at Les Deux Alpes.

*

Menton, on the Med.
Elsewhere, honest autumn.
Here, summer dwindles.
Crones crawl through hurled swash –
Gandhis, Oxfam ads.
Perky young firm bums
and tits grow over-ripe.
Olives darken, fill,
fall on the Tende road.
Once Clicquot was swigged
from their sweet slippers.
Cheap plastic flip-flops,
Labyrinth soles.

Cattle-trucks rev on
the prom, take veal
for the abattoir. Like
a bloodhound's eyes,
flab droops. The breeze
is edged with salt;
tiers of near-dead
leaves shiver, turn
backs on the low sun.

*

In the Château d'Antibes, Musée Picasso:
polyglot coach-hordes reverentially
cluster ten deep and peer at, from two inches,
doodles, framed opulently in wrought gilt,
which (in Italian, French, German and English)
a Guide tries desperately to justify.
'This is a Post-Synthetic Cubist work.
Poseidon *with his trident* is a symbol.
Here, *Form* and *Image* matter more than *Likeness*.'
(Vague crap, the sort they tell you on Pre-Dip.)
Perplexed suburban mums, despairing fraus,
middle-aged middle-class Europe huddles up
united in its mutual dazed wonder
at how an alien culture could creep on
and overtake it in its own lifetime.
A dozen Japs behind Yashikas enter,
grinning incredulous bewilderment.
Twelve flashes (doubtless for projection later
in front of supercilious Tokyo smirks).
The oldest has a young girl at his side
(who holds hands with an English-looking bloke)
and scrutinises marks where paint has drooled,
then whispers to her. Bright gold fillings glint.
'Grandfather say of Art of East and West
"Sometimes is interesting, sometimes a puzzle,
sometimes is" – how the English say? – "slipshod".'

*

Camping Provençal. Notices: (1)
Tourists may only settle in the camp,
after if having checked in at the office
they know their places. (2) The campers' dresses
must be correct in camp. (3) Please no noise
between the 22 and seven-o-clock.
(4) In the camp, parents must watch across
their children. (5) Take care of the plantations,
don't set up nails nor pour dish-water on
the trees. (6) Fire-woods are forbidden. (7)
Linen must dry discretely. (8) Detritus,
put this into the dustbins. (9) Showers-bath,
wash-house and W.C. must be kept clean.
Water is quite uncommon in Provence.
(10) Management is NOT responsible
for thefts. (11) Speed don't exceed 5.
(12) *That* box is reserved alone for throw
sanitary-towels and periodicals.
(13) These rules must be respected under
penalty of your time expiring here.

*

When I went it was Saturday. Les Grottes
de Niaux are Sunday-opening. A tight
steel door, as to a bank vault, locked away
graffiti twenty thousand years (approx)
of age. But I had seen it on a carte
postale illustrée – bison speared, vague blot
of antelope.* Quite fascinating? Yes,
because of something other than good art.

A Zeppelin dick in felt-tip stains the rocks.

To aid the hunt? To work off horniness?
Partly, no doubt. And partly both convey,
and partly were inspired by, mortal fright.

*

* *I have subsequently learned that wild horses, not
antelopes, feature in the cave paintings at Niaux.*

This is where Bernadette
visioned the Virgin and wet
  herself (1858)
  and the distempered congregate –
Iron Lungs, Kidney Machines, crutches –
confidently, for such is
  the miraculous property of the Spring
  that a few swigs cure anything
(with the notable omission
of Catholic superstition).

Concrete is glib, gleams with generations
of pilgrims' melted candle-wax which
Municipal workers scrape up. A nutter
caresses the cave wall, gives it French kisses.
Multi-lingual Masses every
15 minutes. Knick-knack emporia –
plastic bottles for the magic water,
3D cards of the grotte. From the rock
crutches dangle, Maria simpers.
Factory girls as they pass get down
on the knees of torn tights, kiss tarmac (icy
at 8 a.m.). The afflicted amass.
Rosary-fumbling parents of
a child who is (predictably, since
they must have been over 40 when
the happy event took place) a Mongol.
Precocious of me, I know, but: 'Irreverence
is a greater oaf than Superstition'?,
W.H.A., *really!*

Dr Cooper's Story

A friend of mine, Dr Edward Cooper,
received a parcel postmarked INTERCOURSE
(which, it seems, is in Pennsylvania)
and – not knowing anyone in that place,
and politics being what they are now –
took it to the local Police Station
to inform the Force of his suspicion
that the package was a bomb. A Sergeant
thanked Dr Cooper profusely and said
he would cause the parcel to be looked at
by Bomb Disposal Squad experts in Crewe.
Some days later a phone call from the same
Sergeant reassured Dr Cooper that
Bomb Disposal Squad experts had 'cleared' the
item in question. A further visit
to the Police Station procured the parcel
which now had a little window cut in it
through which a tiny periscope had been
insinuated establishing that
the contents were four small pots of jam.
No letter had been enclosed to explain
the identity of the donor and
my friend has never subsequently
found out who sent the jam – which he says was
the tastiest he has ever eaten.

Address Protector

My wife's remark, that in her mother's day
a phenomenon existed called the Dress
Protector, interested me – until
I found she hadn't said *Address* Protector

(I'd been re-reading *Work Suspended* and felt
sympathy for Plant's father's all-transcending
'aloofness that was his dominant concern
in life' – what could be more God-sent than this
Address Protector to repel assaults
from pesky impertinent acquaintances?).
Alas, Technology's not that advanced yet.
The Dress Protector was, it seems, a pad
against the stains from sweaty under-arms.

Aloofness is not that easily achieved –
Plant's father, who specialised in painting weird
pictures intended for no audience,
said 'Only Philistines like my work and,
by God, I like only Philistines' (but he
found himself horridly acclaimed *recherché*
and, irony of ironies, *sought-after*).

I know (no names/no pack-drill) of a drunk
who seeks unconsciousness because he can't
stomach his fellow-men: but when he drinks
he strikes up new acquaintanceships – which means
more twerps to seek escape from the next night...

Alternative Communities don't work –
everyone now lives in some clapped-out farmhouse
with weaving on a *real* Indian loom
and dung-grown carrots that you have to talk to
with love to make them extra full of *goodness*
and hand-thrown coffee-mugs with shit-brown glazes
and stone-ground flour and Whatsisname just back
from being a Transcendentalist (goose-fleshed
under a shaved pate in un-English drag)
– no, loonies were ever far too *numerous.*

Aloofness is not that easily achieved.
Colt's is the only foolproof way yet known.
So be a sweety, Technological Man,
apply your wit to this – one would prefer
a (Pat. Pend.) vinyl-coated digital
Address Protector to an ounce of lead.

Eavesdropped

1

'Jim was a lark today in The Rose & Crown
(he's in Show Business, compères comedy turns
at Pontin's in Prestatyn in the Season).
"Talking of Bingo," he said "how would it be
if Tommy Cooper was the Caller? Listen:
'All right now, ladies and gents, here's five and four,
that's nine – just like that!' " (Counting his fingers like.)
"Or Ken Dodd: 'All right Missus, Lucky For Some,
that's fifteen – lucky for *some* I said, hard luck,
it's not your lucky day – tattybye Missus!'
Or an old Jew Boy: 'Three and nine already,
that's thirty-nine already but, vell, to *you*
it's *tventy*-nine.' " Yes, Jim was a lark today
in The Rose & Crown. I thought "When the wife asks
'Had a good time love?' I'll be able to say
'Jim was a lark today in The Rose & Crown...' " '

2

'No kiddies! You'll regret it when you're old.
I always say "Thank God I've got my three" –
course Viv, my second, married last July
(she's got a darling baby boy and now
I'm knitting woollies ready for another).
Our Alec's wife's had four (Alec's Viv's brother).
Our Myrtle's still at school – she's going to try
for Office Work if she gets CSE.
"Kiddies are an investment for old age,"
I always say. They oughtn't to allow
this Women's Liberance that's all the rage.
Have some, or you'll regret it when you're old.'

'MORE BLOODY VERMIN HERE NOW THAN THERE'S PEOPLE!'

(an usherette of a Sheffield cinema
informs a passing sandwich-board-man as she
bursts out of foyer doors holding a shovel,
on which reposes a moribund black rat
with one red bubble slung from each shut nostril.
Little bones crackle as she tamps it between
too-narrow cast iron bars of a drain in
the kerb. To which he replies)

'Yer wah?'

'I said
"MORE BLOODY VERMIN HERE NOW THAN THERE'S PEOPLE!"'

CUT COSTLY RESEARCH!

is aerosoled on
the Chemistry Wing.
VIVA RESEARCHERS!
say I. Long may my
heroes pay homage
to what ennobles
sapiens man – the
great non-mystery
of what is conceived
by puny us to
be mysterious.

SOMETHING FOR EVERYONE!!!

HERE COMES SENSATIONAL
CIRCUS APOLLO!
FIRST EVER VISIT TO
SHEEP SALES FIELD, LUDLOW!

BROUGHT HERE FROM FRANCE,
LES PUPPETEERS!
FEATURING, YES!,
THE 18 INCH STRONG MAN!
GONZALEZ WITH CHARIOT,
ACTING THE GOAT!
MISS BARBARELLA'S
ABOUNDING HOUNDS!
FRECKLES THE FIRE HORSE!
OSTRICH & FRIEND!
MISS GINA, CONTORTIONS!
MANIPULATION
EXTRAVAGANZA
BY J.J. MARRIOTT!
IVANO'S AERIAL
BALANCE SENSATION!
FIRST TIME IN BRITAIN,
ILLUSION SUPREME,
MARC CHRISTIAN SAWS
THE LADY IN HALF!
FLY HIGH WITH SEXY
MISS DEBBIE SUE!

FINALLY: CLOWNS,
ALANDO & LOUI,
PLUS DAVIE DUCK
& MICKY MONKEY! –
WHEN YOU'VE SEEN *THEM*,
LAUGH?, YOU'LL SIMPLY DIE!

Nothing For Anyone

Cancel our Dailies and Monthlies.

Population, Energy, Food.
The present United Nations
Forecast of Population
for year 2000 is over
7,000 millions.
Lord Ashby spells it out for us *
(*Encounter*, March '76) –
for Western Industrial Man
this isn't just another
crisis but a climacteric.

Less weighty, a Sunday Sup.
reports on Alcoholism.

The Art Correspondent, clearly,
don't know his Arp from his Albers.

In Essex, I read, there are more
ponies per square stockbroker's
daughter than anywhere else.

This sot's liver – a metaphor
for sterling's swollen decease
and Technological Man
and before him Roman, Mayan,
Minoan, all *Homo erectus*
and what he conceives as Cosmos
in his own petty perspective
blown oversize by an ego
too big to survive itself.

(What else but dummies like us
could aim for 'More motor cars
to put us back on our feet'?)

**A Second Look at Doom*, by Eric Ashby, *Encounter*, Vol. XLVI, No.3.

Some snivelling Celt reviews verse.
Compared with De Witts' Black Holes,†
a handful of weighed syllables
has no future (nor has future).

ALBERT, ONE HUNDRED TODAY,
ATTRIBUTES HIS FITNESS TO 'X' –
A LIFE-DRUG KNOWN ONLY TO HIM!
(One is reminded of Ferret
in Smollett's *Launcelot Greaves*
'...this here Elixir of Long Life,
if properly used, will protract
your days till you shall have seen
your country ruined.')

                Of course
it will still take us by surprise –
nine out of ten oafs in the street,
a census informs me with cheer,
fondly imagine we'll find
deposits of copper and oil
ad nauseam, or find substitutes.
Possibly; possibly not.
Meanwhile, CIPEC and OPEC
won't *give* it away, we will pay –
or, atavistically, war.

As the Leisure Pages observe,
EARLY RETIREMENT IS COMING.

If ever the headlines strike home,
and they see there's nothing to lose,
the nine out of ten will run riot
as these on the Sports Page – terraces
dripping with apes' blood (the same
lovelies, I think, who enriched
the bogs with the following legend
HEADBUTTS AND BOOTS IS OUR BIZNUSS
SHAGGERS IS RULERS OK?) –

† *Black Holes*, edited by Cecile De Witt and Bryce S. De Witt
(Gordon & Breach, 1974)

yes, add to the cumulate threats,
amassing at x to the nth,
insurrection civil and bloody –
Homo erectus autophagous.

F.T. Index down 1 p.c.
Frankly, we couldn't care less.

Never let it be said that *we*
ever stood in the way of regress.

10 x 10 x 10

One winter evening, Donald travelled the
15 miles to his girlfriend's home town and,
disliking her parents, decided to
phone her house and arrange to rendezvous
at the end of her road rather than call
for her and have to face her mum and dad.
Her mother answered the phone and said that
Susan was visiting a friend nextdoor.
'Where are you ringing from?' 'Oh, I'm at home.'
(He was, in fact, only round the corner.)

Having put down the phone, he decided
to walk to the house nextdoor to Susan's,
collect her from there and go to the pub
(thus still avoiding her parents). He set
off along the road where the kiosk was
and, after a few minutes, turned at right
angles into Susan's road and sauntered
towards her friend's; when all of a sudden
out of the pitch darkness bounded a dog
which he recognised as Sue's Dalmatian.

A distant street-light illumined a pair,
identified by Don as Sue's parents
(which identification was confirmed
by her mother's voice shouting 'Heel, Measles!' –
he well knew both voice and nomenclature).
Rightly judging that they might find it odd
to encounter one who had telephoned
only five minutes ago and told them
emphatically that he was 15 miles
distant, he panicked and turned on his heel.

He walked briskly away from them, but thought,
as he passed under a sodium light,
that they might recognise him, so he hunched
his back – hoping thus to disguise his frame.
He lacked confidence in this, however,
and to consolidate his disguise he
affected a limp – first left leg, then right.
Thus, alternating legs, he limped faster
and faster away from her parents, till
he was limp-sprinting at 10 m.p.h.

But Measles, who knew him, tore after him,
yelping and biting his trouser leg. 'Down,
bad Measles!' he whispered between clenched teeth
while oscillating extravagantly.
He paused at the corner, smacked Measles' snout,
said 'Damn and blast it all to bloody Hell!',
ran his fastest (unhampered by Measles
and now using conventional techniques)
and thought 'This could be good to write about –
but in the third person, naturally.'

On another occasion, Donald was
out drinking with a friend when closing time
came, so, wishing to continue their chat,
they went to a theatre which also
had a restaurant serving drinks till 12.
Drinks were only served to people dining
and, not wanting anything to eat, Don
went to the bar for two pints of bitter.
'No drinks without meals, sir.' 'Oh, we've just got
our meal, over on that table.' he lied.

'You're a bloody liar – you've only just
come in. Get out. You're not getting served.' So
he left by one of three doors and went down
a dark corridor. But it must have been
the wrong door, because he found himself in
a huge auditorium – house lights dimmed,
only the stage lights ablaze – completely
deserted. He stumbled along the aisle
to the stage, which he mounted, noticing
a stage *on* the stage – 10 x 10 x 10.

He clambered up to the stage on the stage
and sang Maurice Chevalier numbers,
danced to the empty auditorium.
'Evry leel briz sim to weesper Looiz.
Eef a natingel coo sing lak you. Sank
Even for leetel girls – zey grow up in
ze mos delightfool away. Ooh la la!
Eet is – ow you Eenglish say? – saucy, no?'
Behind him, twenty feet high, he noticed
a catwalk reached by a metal ladder.

He climbed the ladder and danced along the
foot-wide catwalk. 'Evry leel briz sim to' –
suddenly he lost balance and fell but
clutched at the back-drapes to save himself and
thought 'I am an interloper, therefore
I must do nothing to damage this hall.'
Thinking his weight would rip the curtains, he
let go, fell down a few feet, grabbed hold, then
let go again and grabbed hold again till
the fabric began to tear and conscience

forced Don to let go for fear of damage.
*   *   *   *   *   *   *   *   *   *
*   *   *   *   *   *   *   *   *   *
*   *   *   *   *   *   When he regained
consciousness, he was considering the
arbitrary nature of the Sonnet –
'One might as well invent any kind of
structure (ten stanzas each of ten lines each
of ten syllables might be a good one),
the subject-matter could be anything.'

Zygmunt

They call Zygmunt Ciggy because he smokes
60 a day. 18 stone. 6 feet 6.
Pole refugee. Abattoir-man. The blokes
mimic his 'z' for 'th' and play tricks
on him – like one day they locked the door
of the Killing Shed with only a mad
Angus and Ciggy inside. 'Why for
you do zis to me?' he yelled. They had
no need to slaughter the beast – spattered gore
stained Zygmunt's forearms a fortnight.

Queer,
that today in the pub it signifies more,
as his wife wheels him in, that he asks for beer
not vodka, than that his mirthless answer
to 'Why for zey do zis to you?' is 'Cancer'.

The Con Men

It isn't that we care about the *Hippo*,
but that we want our children's children's children
to see it for their entertainment.

It's
our children's children's children precisely who
make the extinction of the Hippo (and
themselves) inevitable.

To have devised
a Theory of Evolution, yet
to imagine *we* remain somehow outside
its sensible advance, has been our costly
luxury up till now; and 'Conservation'

meant *what a shame the kiddies got slick-oil*
between their toes on seaside holidays
or *Save the Hippo!* (for Safari coach-trips),
replaced now by the *sapiens* conceit
that somehow we must organise our course
of Evolution to preserve *ourselves!*
(unable to accept that nasty 'Nothing',
we long ago evolved the comfy Spook).

The Ant inside the Test Zone (that 'survived,
despite exposure to large overdoses')
and *Penicillium* and Stone and Vacuum
are queuing up impatiently behind.

The only thing it matters to is us.

Receipt (1793)

For Cancer – boil some finest Turkey figs
in newest milk, applying them as hot
as can be scarcely borne onto the Cancer
which must be washed 11 times a day
in the milk (warmed). The figs must be applied
fresh in the morning, once or twice by day
and in the night. The quantity of figs –
to be boiled up each time, to be proportioned
unto the size of that place to be covered.
The use of this cure must be persevered in
for 3 or 4 months. An old man was cured
of most inveterate Cancer (which began
festering at one corner of his mouth,
had eat clean thro' his cheek and half way down
his throat) with only six pounds of best figs.
A woman was, in the like manner, cured,
being afflicted ten years with a Cancer.

Her breast was used to bleed so exceedingly
that it was by the Faculty supposed
to be an ulcer. By repeating figs
three times, it stopped – employing only 12
pounds of best Turkey figs. First application
of the said poultice is attended with
a deal of pain, but after that the patient
finds ease and much relief with every fresh one.
To cure the Cancer if inveterate,
eat only turnips boiled and turnips' liquor.
At these times, you don't drink the milk, nor have
no beer, wine or spirits, which inflames
the blood that by the Cancer is inflamed –
a person was of Rheumatism cured,
another of the Scurvey in two months
with this most efficacious mode of living
and air and exercise which cleared the blood
of all unclean inflammatory heat.
For Hectic Fever and for Spitting Blood,
Consumption on the lungs et cetera –
bleeding is serviceable, and a diet
of Whorehound Plantain mixed in Buttermilk
in the fresh vapours of some country town.
A person was by this receipt quite cured
of Heart Affliction, sometimes called Love Gout.

FICTION

(1979)

(Verse is <u>not</u> Fiction –
ask any librarian.)

Fiction

Donald is a fictitious character
arrived at an age and bodily state
rendering suicide superfluous,
would rather sip Grands Crus than throw his leg.
He is a writer of fiction. He says
'Even one's self is wholly fictitious.'
Hatred once drew him to satiric verse
but he could think of nothing to rhyme with
'Manageress of the Angel Hotel',
or 'I call my doctor *"Killer" Coldwill'*
(a fictitious name, 'Coldwill', by the way),
or 'Headmaster of the Secondary Mod.'

Donald has created a character
called 'Donald' or 'Don' who keeps a notebook
dubbed *Donald's Spleneticisms,* e.g.:
'Complacent as a Country Town GP ',
'Contemptible as County Council Clerks',
'A hateful little Welshman shared my train
with no lobes to his ears and yellow socks',
'Seedy as Salesmen of Secondhand Cars'.

In Donald's novel, 'Don' writes poetry –
titles such as 'It's a Small World', 'Fiction',
'Y – X', 'Remaindered', which he sends
to literary periodicals
under the nom de plume *'Peter Reading'*
(the present writer is seeking advice
from his attorney, Donald & Donald).
This fictitious bard has a doctor called
'Coldwill' who sleeps with the manageress
of the Angel (and sues 'Don' for libel).

In Donald's novel, 'Don' (whose nom de plume
is *'Peter Reading'*) sues a man whose *real*
name is 'Peter Reading' for having once
written a fiction about a poet
who wrote verse concerning a novelist
called 'Donald' whose book *Fiction* deals with 'Don'
(a poet who writes satirical verse
and is sued by an incompetent quack,
the manageress of a pub, a Celt
with lobeless ears and yellow socks, acned
Council clerks and a Range Rover salesman).

In 'Reading's' fiction, the poet who writes
verse concerning the novelist 'Donald'
is sued by the latter who takes offence
at the lines '... an age and bodily state
rendering suicide superfluous,
would rather sip Grands Crus than throw his leg'.
For the Defence, 'Donald, QC' says that
'Even one's self is wholly fictitious.'

Early Morning Call

At 3 this morning there is light enough to see
that the steam squeezed from this pasture and the
mist veiling holiday mornings when you were a boy
are no different; curlews employ
the same diatonic now as then. No, the difference is
        that the same phenomena don't have the same impact.
It is chilling to suddenly grasp the very simple fact
that you do not feel as *well* as then,
nor, you may be sure, ever will again.

It's a Small World

Wayne meets Jayne outside the Nip Embassy
which both are haranguing because, it seems,
WHOLESALE WHALE MASSACRE BY JAPS MUST STOP!!

Later, in the All Wheat Restaurant, Jayne says
'Yeah, Tolkien's fine, but have you read *Shardik*?
Great!' (This is way back in '76.)

Wayne thongs Jayne an amorphous wallet thing
(he is into leathercraft) and, guess what? –
they both *think* for five minutes each morning.

Both are into getting an Orkneys croft
when they finish Tech. Wayne visits Jayne's mum's
at Bromley – 'Tarot cards, great! *And* joss-sticks!'

You may not believe this, but it turns out
that Jayne's mum knew Wayne's dad back in '60.
(How was he? Was he a Friend of the Earth?

They'd met on the Aldermaston whatsit.
In Trafalgar Square the Fascist Pigs had
picked them up, still cross-legged, and booked them both.)

Proposed Increases

Up 25p – simple lettering,
up 50p – endurance-suitable stone,
up 50p – 3 feet in depth, up 10p –
to 90p six feet in depth, up 10p –
upkeep, up 70p – ministers' fees,
up 75p – (in non-purchased ground)
the actual laying-in (in purchased ground,
up 90p), up 10p – right to erect.
Rate for a stillborn child remains unchanged.
A spokesman said: 'As prices go these days,
this is considered more than reasonable.'

Y – X

X daily drove the 7.15 from Stretton.
Y, whom he shared the task with, remarks this:
'Six foot, ee were, ex-pug. Sometimes eed *stare*...
– but mostly, like, ee seemed like any other
bloke (but they always do) – eed put a bet on
and, Satdy nights, used to get on the piss.
Lived, since I knowd im, with is crippled mother.
– Angd isself dressed in ladies' underwear.'

5

Livid green fingers
quarter a two-inch
disc (3 a.m.). Dark.
Grid of window-frame
on the wall throbs blue.

...tickticktickticktick-
tickticktickticktick...
Klaxon: eee-ow, *eee-
ow*, eee-ow, *eee-ow*,
EEE-OW, *EEE-OW*. Brakes.

Aromatic mint.
When inhalation
suddenly ceases,
a yearn for scent of
household-dust even.

Peppermint tablet
reduces to chalk.
Though bitter, each grain
at the last moment
is sweet to the tongue.

Fretfully twisted
grip of moist bed-sheet
in senile fist helps
relieve a weight like
wet sand-bag on chest.

*

Kingfisher-blue light
each second. White door.
Scarlet cross. Black flask
labelled O_2. Black
peaked cap. One-way glass.

...RESPIRATORY.
WILCO. HASTENING
(BLEEP; BLEEP) CASUALTY
ALL SPEED. MESSAGE TIMED
O THREE SEVENTEEN...

Vying with Dettol,
nicotine wafts from
ambulance-man's hands
each side my bald head.
Rubber oxygen.

Sometimes demotic
is also precise
viz: mouth now tastes like
the bottom of a
budgerigar's cage.

As if tight thonging
bound the diaphragm.
Itchy coarse blanket.
The palm sweaty of
someone's hand held tight.

Sir, in flannel bags,
beckoning boys in.
Eyes, blurred with speed, note
Higgo's black toe-cap
stuck out. Ground rises.

Roar: *TWO-FOUR-SIX-EIGHT,*
WHO-DO-WE-AP-REE-
CI-ATE? C-O-L-
L-E-G-I-A-
T-E, COLLEGIATE ! ! !

Spearmint. First mowings
off the Games Field. School-
Meals-Service-van-stink.
Earth, pungent sphagnum.
Metallic blood reek.

Beech Nut chewy. Then
grate of sour grit/ sweet
shoots of spring grass. Then
nasal blood swallowed,
cupric – of pence sucked.

Stitch under ribs aches.
Sucked air sore on lungs.
Ground battering soles.
Knees, muzzle, chest, palms,
smashed concurrently.

*

Close-up of boob in
flotsam of torn-off
tights, pants; beyond which
3 a.m. shows on
the travelling-clock.

Purr of a zip. Moan.
Rustle. A hiss of
silk stroked. A gasp. Quick
deep inhalation.
Regular squelch. Quiet.

Sabaean parfum
des arbres singuliers,
verts tamariniers,
des fruits savoureux.
Cheesy pudenda.

Colgate with fluoride.
Slurping tongues, after
an hour, remind one
of well-hung partridge
(followed by Roquefort).

Opulent soft flesh
cool on belly and
thighs concurrently.
Painful release/ bliss –
a bit like a sneeze.

Polished steel basin
containing lancets
mirrors crow's-feet. Cup
clamped on nose and mouth.
Ensoresque mask leers.

Steel trolley clatters.
Gush, as of Ocean
heard in a shell, falls;
rises; falls; rises;
falls. A voice gasps 'Christ!'

Meths, Dettol, laundered
linen, TCP,
PVC, rubber.
Sinus contracts to
vinegar, copper.

Viscid foul spit. Plaque
licked from my own tongue
tastes of overhung
game or Bombay Duck.
Suddenly cupric.

Throb of a tube in
larynx and gullet.
Pressure of tight mask
pinching the muzzle.
Sheet scrapes over pate.

And Now, a Quick Look at the Morning Papers

lled in
    ar smas
e freed b
    iremen from the wreckage of his Ren
fter both had been in collision wit
    hrysler Avenger. The A49 was blocke
en to cut both drivers from their v
    dition of the other driver as 'sati
rsday – the day after his fiftiet
    or alcohol proved positive, a p
juries to his head and left l
    mproving' said a hospital o
lso certified dead was Do
    eaves a wife and two chi
aid 'He just drove ou
    othing I could do.'
Parochial Church
    early retire
any year
    fini
ha

Festival

The Aeolian String Quartet
is coming to strum in the church
of *this very picturesque town.*
King Lear done in dirty macs
in the grounds of the Norman castle.
The usual Festival freaks –
Alternative Technologists
(to wit: advocates of tiny
windmills and solar roof tiles –
well-meaning Spike Milligan types),
ladies in synthetic fur
(no one, nowadays, wants to harm
those cuties the stoats and the sables)
who like art a lot once a year.

*

There is an exhibition of photographs by a young Derbyshire
gentleman. He has just finished a Fine Art (Photography) course
at a provincial college and been given a thousand pounds by the
Arts Council. An American institution has offered him seven
thousand dollars for fifteen folios of snaps. He is naive, which is
inexcusable, and ill-informed, which is tiresome. He does not know
the title of his newly-conferred qualification; he has not heard of Mr
Charles Osborne; he has not had the civility to acquaint himself
with the name of his American benefactor. He says 'Art is a struggle'
(the u as in 'cuckoo'). I say 'Thanks to the Arts Council of Great
Britain, it has been no struggle so far; thanks to the unknown
American foundation, it will be no struggle for a while.' He says
'My father's a miner.' I believe I evince no awe. He continues
'When he let me go to college he made me promise it was on the
condition that it wouldn't change me at all.' I am able to reassure
him.

*

A minor Thespian, off duty from *'Lear,* asks the barman for a Drambuie, a Crème de Menthe, a Curaçao, a Benedictine, a green Chartreuse, a yellow ditto, a Cointreau, a Cherry Brandy, a Kirsch and a Crème de Cacao in a half-pint tumbler. 'Four pounds fifty six, please Sir. A unusual drink, Sir, if I may say so.' The Thespian, sipping the subfusc fluid, sighs 'I always drink it. Tastes exactly like draught Guinness.'

*

On the First Night, the Thespians
(who really *do* say *'Darling,*
haven't seen you for *ages!'*)
have drinkies at the local.
Ladies who love art abound,
there is even one from Noo Joysey
whom Donald puzzles by saying
'You speak no French, Madam? A shame.
You see, I speak no North American.'
She asks does he 'understand art'.
'(Mon cul.) Oui, je comprends bien –
l'Art c'est un fauve trop sauvage
pour attaquer de front tout seul;
il faut toujours chercher l'Art
avec une troupe de chasseuses.'

An Everyday Story of Countryfolk

Whenever anyone was killing a
pig, she would buy (they called her Pig Susie)
chitterlings, brains, blood, for a shilling a
bucketful. Married to the big, boozy
owner of the Glebe Farm, she nursed, in nine
years, eight children. Her black puddings and brawn
sustained them – bowls of brains immersed in brine
littered the kitchen like bowls of frog spawn.
    One evening, as she came from a neighbour's
with an apronful of pig guts, her man,
drunk from the Plough after his day's labours,
knocked her down with his bike. When she began
scraping the apron's contents up, poor bloke,
thinking he'd disembowelled her, had a stroke.

Choreograph

High-rise of thirty storeys, thirty
windows on each storey, of which this
window opposite, three metres square,
reveals nine only, each three metres
square, each an individual's cell.

^{1}A	^{2}B	^{3}C
^{4}D	^{5}E	^{6}F
^{7}G	^{8}H	^{9}I

TO LET on windows 4, 5 and 6.
4 devoid of furniture, only
one roll of bright red linoleum
to which D strenuously applies
himself with a very large hammer
and small nails picked from between the lips.

E, in white overall, rolls green paint
on wall separating 5 from 6.

F, in blue overall, rolls brown paint
on wall separating 6 from 5.

B removes comb from pocket, combs hair,
rises from desk, removes jacket, hangs
jacket on door between offices
2 and 3, enters thus office 3.

G puts fingers in ears and glowers
at ceiling where fluorescent fitting
flashes on and off once per second
then cuts out leaving 7 obscure.

A turns as door between 2 and 3
closes, rises from desk and enters
office 2 by door interjoining
1 and 2, moves to door between 2
and 3, removes, from jacket of B,
copious wallet, which is replaced
after extraction of notes therefrom.
A returns, via door between 1
and 2, to 1 and, reseated, writes.

H works finger up nose with leisured
thoroughness of assured privacy.

C, as B enters 3, spins round from
cabinet, where files are being filed,
rushes towards B, who closes door
between 2 and 3 and places chair
at angle against door. Arms like coils,
white garment slides from shoulder of C,
three metres square Venetian-blind falls.

I, slouched over office 9's desk, may
be generously assumed asleep.

You Can't Be Too Careful

Reports, unfortunately, indicate
Warble infections reaching record peaks.

Statistics from the 1974
National Survey show 40%
Fluke infestation of the British Isles.

Nematodirus could be with us SOON! –
our drench eliminates this deadly worm!

Fluke may have been ingested since September:
this can be countered using Flukanide.

Beware of ORF! Eliminate Grass Staggers!
By treating NOW eradicate those Warbles!

Where Swayback has occurred before, inject
(do not give orally) in pregnancy.

Spray NOW with Cobalt Sulphate – prevent Pine!

Where Worm Burden is evident, e.g.
Scouring or marked Unthriftiness etc.,
drench physically or use granules or dust.

Treat Bowel & Stomach Worm with Bovicam!

It is COMPULSORY to dip for SCAB!
Control Scab AND Mycotic Dermatitis!

Use added CHLORFENVINPHOS to protect
against Fly Strike (also Lice, Keds and Ticks).

No danger of abortion with THIS liquid!

Spray this solution freely on all parts –
especially legs, face and genitals.

Don't let Lungworm Husk catch *you* unawares!

Madamooselle – A Conversation

(Old Man/ Keith/ Babby)

O.M.   I'll fight you. 'll you fight me?

B.   Keith'll fight you. He'll knock you down.

O.M.   He'll knock *you* down.

B.   No, *you*.

O.M.   He'll lay one on ya.

B.   No, on *you*.

K.   We'll sell you.

O.M.   Yeah, we'll sell you when yose gets older.

K.   Get a lot of money for you.

O.M.   Do you want to go to school?

B.   Na.

K.   You'll go to school soon.

O.M.   Yeah, you'll go to school.

K.   Don't you want to go to school?

B.   Na.

O.M.   Well you'll go.

B.   Keith'll knock you down.

K.   Do you want to buy a babby?

O.M.   Sent our daughter to Madamooselle.

K.   The French lady?

O.M.   Yeah.
        Would she go to school? Nah. Scream 'er would.
        Scream. Soon as 'er got in that push-chair, scream.

K.   Wouldna go to school.

O.M.   This 'n 'll scream.

K.   Yar'll scream when yer go to school, 'll yer?

O.M.   Yeah, I can tell.
        Sent our daughter to the French lady.
        Pity 'er got murdered.

Inter-City

He reads 'But the most unusual thing
about him is his teeth. They are dentures
but they are not ivory. They're made of
some sort of metal, some say steel, others
Duralumin. Anyway, they give him
a somewhat sinister appearance when
he shows them, as he does when he smiles.' He
replaces the book* in his slimline brief-
case and produces *Pun & Ink (The Life
of Thomas Hood)* which he pretends to read.

A newly-arrived fellow-passenger
attempts the *Guardian* crossword for five
minutes then says 'Excuse me, put I can't
help noticing se pook you're reating. You
atmire sat biographer, to you?' A
monocle magnifies one cobalt eye.
'I *am* that biographer,' lies Donald.
'I take it you've heard of me?' 'Heart of you!
I haf stutiet you altogeser! Please,
I am Liebgarten, Doctor Liebgarten.'

Patent heels click. 'Particularly I
atmire your ferse translation of Kokur
Niznegorsky's heroic anthem *The
Soya Bean Canning-Plant Operative,*
vitch, I unterstant, you hat to smuggle
out of its country of origin in
your untervear. *Norna of Fitful-head –
Her Influence on Ted Hughes's Later
Style* also I like. Tell me, vot are you
going to write apout in se next von?'

---

* *Biggles Takes a Holiday* by Captain W.E. Johns.
Hodder & Stoughton 1949.

'I have in mind the story of a chap
who went to work in the kitchens of a
celebrated West End hotel – washing
dishes, cooking breakfasts, cleaning ovens,
scrubbing floors, assisting the Assistant
Chef and suchlike quite disagreeable
activities. Having for some months held
this respectable position, he fell
into the habitual practice of
filching his Sunday supper from the fridge.

This hebdomadary beano was quite
contrary to the expectations of
the establishment – which, whilst providing
nourishment for employees, neglected
the sophisticated requirements of
our hero. He purchased, from Berry Bros.
& Rudd, a case of halves of Clos de Bèze
1961 to accompany
the cold roast partridge purloined each Sabbath.
Soon the game was up. The management guessed.

A padlock was put on the coldstore door
and he was summoned to the manager's
office. "Now then, Donald," the manager
said, "to be perfectly honest with you,
over the last few weeks a number of
items have gone missing out of the fridge.
What do you think of that?" "I am shocked, sir,
deeply deeply shocked." "So are we. That's why
we've decided to entrust you alone
of all our under-staff with the fridge key."

Until the first day of February
(the end of the partridge shooting season)
no Sunday passed without *Perdix perdix*
enhancing our hero's willow-pattern.'
'Pravo! Unt I am remintet now of
a man like your Tonalt who vent to vork
se kitchen of a restaurant in Soho.
First in se morning his jop vas to mop
se floors – who vas alvays covert in grease
especially rount se foot of se stove.

153

Vell, in se kitchen corner vas kept a
fire extinguisher on se floor, unt von
morning vile mopping he picket it up
to mop petter in se corner. Vell, he
replact se fire extinguisher ven he
hat moppt put it vas a preak-pottle type
unt se force of his putting it town must
have proken se pottle – Achtung! he cries
unt foam is schpurting everyvere unt he
picks up se frightful sing in alarm unt

turns arount looking for somevere to schvirt
it harmlessly. Alas! on se stove is
a four foot long salmon poaching gently.
Vooosh! it is coatet in five inch of fizz.
Schpinning rount in fright, still holting se fire
extinguisher, he fizzes se Het Chef.
Soon he is packing his pags unt leaving.'
Laughter, then five minutes silence follows.
'Soon you are reaching your testination!
You see how kvickly your journey passes!

Now you vill sign your latest pook for me!'
Hands him a sumptuous work entitled
Dis Quiet, or The Devil's Kitchen in
full polished tree calf, gilt in compartments,
crimson lettering-pieces, dentelles, all
edges uncut, all pages blank, only
the water-mark GARDEN CITY. Train stops.
'Where the Hell is this? Who the Hell are you?'
'I am Liebgarten, Doctor Liebgarten.'
The Doctor smiles, showing his metal teeth.

Parallel Texts

(A bucolic employee of
South Shropshire Farmers Ltd.)

(*The Craven Arms, Stretton
& Tenbury Advertiser*)

You remembers that old boy Marsh?
   – im as lived at Stokesay?
   – forever pickin is nose?
Well, this mornin ees takin
some cattle over the line
(course they got underpass, like,
but also the level crossin
as mostly they uses),
an 7.15 from Stretton
runs over the fucker
– course kills im, like, never
you seen such a mess, cows an all.
Still, it dunna matter a lot
– ee were daft as a coot.

A Stokesay farmer was killed
when he was struck by a train
on a stretch of track near
Craven Arms. He was Mr John
Jeremiah Marsh, a 60-year-old
bachelor of Stokesay Castle
Farm, and the accident occurred
just yards from his home, at
Stokeswood – an unmanned level
crossing. Mr Marsh is thought
to have been opening the gate.
The train which struck him
was pulling 39 goods wagons
on its way to Carlisle.

Mens Talents in Difcours Shadowed
out by Muficall Inftruments*

Your Drums are blufterers in difcours, that with a loudnefs domineer in publick over men of better fenfe and fill the place with a rattling found: yt hath feldom any wit in it: it's the emptinefs yt makes it found.

The Lute is directly oppofite to the Drum and founds very fweet and low: the Lutonifts are therefore men of a fine genius, great affability and efteemed chiefly by men of good tafte.

The Trumpet hath but 4 or 5 nots and points out to us men that have learned a fmoothnefs of difcours from the polite company they have kept but have fhallow parts and weak judgements: a play houfe, a drawing room, a ball, a vifiting day, are the few nots they are mafters of.

Violins are your lively forward wits that diftinguifh themfelves by yt fharpnefs of their flourifhes.

Your Bafs Viols yt rumbles in ye bottom of the Confort may fignifie men of rough gener who do not love to hear themfelves talk but fometimes break out into an agreeable bluntnefs in company.

*

As for country wits yt talk with great elagunce: of hares: horfes: quickfet hedges: 5 bard gates: double ditches and broken hocks: muft take up with the tittle of an Hunting Horn.

The Bagpipes yt entertains you from morning till night with a repetition of the fame nots are ye dull heavy fellows: ftory tellers that with a perpetuall humming quite tire your patience.

Harpficords yt are a kind of Confort by themfelves are perfons who are mafters of every kind of converfation and can talk of all fubjects: of which kind there are but few.

* Adapted from *D. Donaldfonne His Booke Anno Dom* 1713
in the author's poffeffion.

Your men that talk of nothing but what is melancholly and look upon mirth as criminall fhall be tirmed Paffing Bells.

The mufick of the Flute is the converfation of a mild amiable woman yt fooths the ear and fills it with a gentle kind of mellody as keeps the mind awake without ftartling it: as raifes an agreeable paffion between tranfport and indolence.

The Hautboy is the moft perfect of the Flute fpecies which with all the fweetnefs of found hath a great ftrength and variety of nots. The Hautboy in this fex is as fcarce as the Harpficord in ye other.

*

That woman who fancys herfelf a wit and difpifes the mufick of the Flute as low and infipit and ftrives to entertain with tart obfervations pert fancies and little turns muft be a Flageolet. The Flageolets among their own fex are more efteemed than the Flutes.

The woman that diftinguifhes herfelf by a great many fkittifh nots: affected fqueaks and is more jiggifh than the Fiddle itfelf muft be called a Kitt.

The women with grave cenfures of vice: fupercilious cafts of ye eye and a feeming contempt for lightnefs of converfation diftinguifh themfelves for to be known by the name of that ancient ferious matron-like inftrument the Virginal.

Your young country lady who with a great deal of mirth and innocence diverts the company very agreeably: by the wildnefs of her nots I would have fignified a Lancafhire Hornpipe: your ramps and bording fchool girls fall under this denomination.

A Welch Harp is an inftrument which very much delights in the tunes of ould hiftoricall ballads: by this I would therefore defcribe a lady that talks of pedigrees and defcents and finds herfelf related to almoft every great family in England for which caufe fhe jarrs and is often out of tune in company for want of their due attention to her.

*

She that accompanys her difcours with motions of ye body: toffes of the head: brandifhes of the fan: whofe mufick is loud and mafculine and fets fomeone or other blufhing fhall be a Kettle Drum.

Your larum houfehould fcaulds or impertinent tittle tattles who have no other variety in difcours but that of talking flower or fafter are to be Caftinets or Jews Harps: all tongue.

Confidering how abfolutely neceffary it is that two inftruments which are to play together for life fhould be exactly tund and go in perfect confort with each other: I would propofe matches between the mufick of both fexts according to the following table of marriage

Drum & Kettle Drum
Lute & Flute
Harpficord & Hautboy
Violin & Flageolet
Bafs Viol & Kitt
Trumpet & Welch Harp
Hunting Horn & Hornpipe
Bagpipe & Caftinet
Paffing Bell & Virginal.

In State*

Wedged matchsticks, Visitor,
lurk at the back of
the serene smile.

Set in crystal,
the waxy finger
can touch no trigger,
nor the opulent slipper
trample to be kissed.

Behind: ranks of cut blooms,
and little birds tethered
by tiny golden links.

* From the Spanish of Pedro Ximénez's *Sobre la muerte del generalísimo
el excelentísimo Sr. conde de Torregamberro.*

Clues

28 Down: Shortened grape of Jerez.
Lout under NO SMOKING triangle smokes.
Stationary, but not at a station.
Cows on the railway line? How odd.
Can anyone do 27 Across:
Un pom led me to writer's disguise?
Isn't that Stokesay Castle over there?
How many waggons on that goods train?
Man in British Rail uniform squats
being sick. Anyone know 25 Down:
Toll or fee split softly to hoax?
Blue flash revolves on roof of white vehicle.
Enormous amorphous lump in a blanket.
23 Down: Iberian prof?

Interview

After lunching curiously
as a guest of the Regional Arts
Association and Town Council,
one of the shortlisted applicants
is invited to perjure himself.
An apoplectic alderman
in a cigarette-burnt baggy pin-stripe,
collar thick with crusts of flaked bald scalp,
says 'Donald, we'll be right informal.
We don't stand on no ceremony.
What did you think of your tour of
our New Community Complex?
What aspect did you find most challenging?'
'Miss Finklestein's Bombsite with Rubble, sir.'
'Oh, you mean our Youth Integration
Project conceived by Miss *Weaselberg* –
yes it's marvellous isn't it? That
Adventure Playground cost forty
thousand quid. The Authorities
won't allow it to open because
it's too dangerous for children.'
A weed in a green poplin shirt asks
'What did you think of our Library?'
'I lost contact with your little man
from the Department of Fun & Games
as he was guiding us there, so
I missed it, I fear. I went into
a place called The George, had two gins
and rejoined the group half an hour later.'
'Department of Leisure & Libraries,
I think you mean, *not* Fun & Games.'
A blowzy old bag in a brown hat
flutters mascara and asks
'Do I remember you saying
you come from Kirkby? That's funny –
I used to work there years ago.'
'Remarkable, madam. Was that
before the War?' 'I'm not that old!'
(She pouts and her ears pinken prettily.)

With dreaded inevitability,
the inanest question of all:
'Is there anything *you'd* like to ask *us*?'
'Yes. Whose recherché idea
was having Blue Nun Liebfraumilch
chambré to accompany beef
for lunch at the Grand Hotel?'
The poor apoplectic purrs modestly
'Yes, they do you right proud at the "Grand".'

The First Three Minutes* &c.

Existence without commencement,
wherein, 15,000
million years ago, three
minutes' expansion and cooling,
particle, antiparticle,
electron, positron,
the fashionable quark,
nuclei of hydrogen
and helium, galaxies,
to cut a short story short,
hot gas, molten stone,
sea, a cell, pterodactyl,
Leakey's pals, God, Pyramids,
the Sistine ceiling, Pam Ayres,
absolutely nobody,
the Heat Death, entropy, Black Holes.

Which knowledge is no excuse
to cease behaving like Gentlemen.

The First Three Minutes, A Moden View of the Origin of the Universe
by Steven Weinberg. André Deutsch 1978.

Mystery Story

One day, the scarcely-known poet received the following:

> 'Baudelaire',
> Mill Street,
> Huddersfield.

Dear Mr R*****g,

    I hope you won't mind me writing to you in this way, but I felt I had to, having just read your latest volume of verse recently published by Secker & Warburg, who were kind enough to supply me with your address. Your work was first drawn to my attention by a review in the Times Literary Supplement by Gavin Ewart. I was so impressed by this that I bought a copy next day and read it in one sitting. What can I say? W.H. Auden (the later works of course), Roy Fuller, Philip Larkin, Dylan Thomas, George MacBeth – truly you belong to our magnificent heritage of Great Bards! I have tried without success to get hold of your other books. Are they out of print, perhaps?

    It may be of interest to you to know that I am the Secretary of our local Poetry Club – a very modest group, I can assure you, of amateur poets and versifiers who get together once a fortnight on a Thursday to read to one another and compare notes. Recently we have invited a number of well-known writers to speak to us about their work and to read extracts. So far this year we have listened to Roger Parbett, Edward Lucie-Smith and the novelist Rachael Summers. Next year, I hope, we shall have Jon Silkin and Percy Nicholson. Would you, I wonder, be interested in joining us sometime? We do, of course, pay a modest fee (generally in the region of £10) plus all expenses. Usually the guest speaker is accommodated for the night at the home of one of our members, and my wife and I would be only too happy to put you up should you decide to come – pure selfishness on our part, I can assure you!

    Once again may I express my great admiration for your work and say that I look forward to hearing from you in the near future. I enclose a stamped addressed envelope.

        Yours very sincerely,
          Alfred E. Hound.

Simultaneously covering the likelihood of the letter being from a duper and the unlikely contingency of its being the work of a bona fide lunatic, the scarcely-known poet replied:

Dear Mr Hound,

I am entrusted, during the absence of Mr R*****g, with answering his correspondence.

I feel certain he will be gratified to read your adulatory opinion of his latest volume and am happy to be able to advise you that, as far as I am aware, his previous collections are still in print and, no doubt, available through any reputable bookseller.

I cannot say whether Mr R*****g will be in a position to take up your kind offer of speaking to your local poetry organisation, but upon his return I shall naturally direct his attention to your letter, when he will doubtless be delighted to contact you if he is able to accept.

Once again, I wish to express the deepest gratitude on behalf of Mr R*****g for your favourable and encouraging letter.

Yours faithfully,
Donald Donaldson
(per procurationem P***r R*****g).

Some weeks later, the scarcely-known poet received the following:

Dear Mr R*****g,

Forgive me writing to you again and taking up more of your valuable time, but as I have not heard from you following my earlier letter, I wondered if I might presume even further by suggesting a little meeting. At least this would avoid your having to employ your pen on such mundane matters when it could be used to such good effect elsewhere!

It so happens that my wife and I will be visiting some relatives in Llandrindod Wells next weekend and, as we will be passing close by your town, I wondered if we might call on you with a view to discussing your possible visit to our poetry group in Huddersfield. Even if you cannot find the time to make the journey north, both my wife and I would greatly enjoy a chance to meet you in the flesh, having had up to now only a rather tendentious view of you through your excellent verse. We should hope to call around midday

163

on Saturday, so perhaps we could have a drink with our little chat – I know what poets are!

By the bye, although I am not familiar with your town, I believe it was once the home of the well-known folk-bard and farmer Fred Jordan. Perhaps you know him?

I hope this arrangement meets with your approval as we are both 'dying' to meet you. We look forward to your reply. Perhaps you would be good enough to enclose street directions or, even better, a map.

Yours sincerely,
Alfred E. Hound.

The scarcely-known poet (abstractedly addressing his reply to 'Rimbaud', Mill Street, Huddersfield) answered:

Dear Mr Hound,

Thank you for your recent letter – that which you sent me previously was, I understand, dealt with by Mr Donaldson on my behalf.

I am fascinated to learn that you have relatives in the Welsh place you mention and that your visiting them there will occasion your arrival here at midday on Saturday next.

Since it is my custom to eat lunch at the time you mention, I trust you will not find it unamusing to share my mahogany and claret bottle on that day.

I am not acquainted with the bucolic gentleman, Fred Jervis or Jardine, whom you are anxious to trace.

I possess no maps.

Yrs. &c.
P***r R*****g.

Some days later, this last letter was RETURNED TO SENDER in a POST OFFICE RETURNED POSTAL PACKET No. 449 as UN-DELIVERED FOR REASON STATED – ADDRESS NOT KNOWN. No more was heard of Hound.

That was thirty years ago. The career of the scarcely-known poet is nearly over. Sometimes, in the early hours of the morning, he lies, confronting obscurity, pondering the true identity of Alfred E. Hound.

164

New Start

I am told these men are *the salt of the earth*
   (I cannot testify to their salinity,
   all I can see is they scratch their genitals).
Some may be worse, none can be more disgusting.
   Guttural bucolics ham-philosophise,
   the gormless spout politics 'Them MPs
is thick as shit, thick as shit them MPs.'
   The Porteus Grinder's amplified barking
   shudders dumb maledicts down the Grinder Pit.
Muffs clamped on the head stop eardrums splitting.
   The Blending Plant Man augers feed to three gullets
   yowling for raw materials. Tenebrous
palpable dust hangs, never precipitates:
   lungs draw it down through abrased nasal tissue.
   Some wear hopeless masks: all rattle when they cough.
Boots slip in spat snot: phlegm is perpetual.
   'You'll find it another world here after what
   you've been used to' my guide says to me, and I
to him 'There are more of you here than I thought.'

Opinions of the Press

I am an abrasive wit,
an oasis of intellect.

Of my kind –
and there are not many of my kind –
I am really quite remarkably good.

I am mordant, very mordant.
Satire is clearly one of my gifts.

Out of everyday matters
I fashion urbane jokes.

My evocation of a seedy hotel room
is particularly liked.

Most of me is marked
by a bitter sense of humour.

I am reminiscent of
intellectual paper-games.

I can handle the Long Poem.

I contain some clever rhymes –
e.g. candid/Gran did.

I am a master of the narrative.
I am a master of the descriptive.

I am looked forward to
being heard from in the future.

ON THE OTHER HAND

I do not transcend pain with Poetry.

I am not as mellifluous as Sir John Betjeman.

I am not as good as
a very great number of people
(who do the same thing better).

Not all of me makes you laugh aloud
on the number 17 bus.

I am drab rhythmless demotic.

I am all very amusing in my way, maybe,
(and definitely mordant)
but am I Art?

Remaindered

Hwaet! When he went,
this provincial sod,
was missed by a wife,
or two other women –
Bordeaux Crus Classés
ironies overnight.
a conveyor cutely
from kid-glove curate
Shelves reel under him,

as hordes will one day,
who some say poeticised,
a mother and one
no workmates spilt tears.
inclined in his bins became
Inching in overdrive,
carted him coolly
to first-class kiln gate.
remaindered unsaleable.

NOTES

Fiction: line 15, '...Donald's Spleneticisms...': In addition to those cited, mention should be made of the following:

Manageress of the Angel Hotel	sulky trollop barge-like feet rhino in a corset brash vache

'Angel Hotel' may refer to an old coaching establishment in a South Shropshire Market Town, or may be wholly fictitious.

Appended to the 'Spleneticisms' is a pp.4 holograph ms. headed <u>2nd</u> <u>Class</u> <u>Singles</u>, of which only the penultimate page is legible, apparently retailing the conversation of a couple in a train – their speech patterns corresponding with the rhythm of the wheels on the railway lines (presumably before the advent of continuous section railway track, when fish-plates interrupted the smooth progress of the wheels, causing a regular, pleasing syncopation):

> '...Why don't you take your hat off?
> Don't you want to take your hat off?
> You could put it on the bag-rack,
> it would only take a minute.
> Would you rather keep your hat on?
> Please yourself, then, keep your hat on.
> If you wanted, you could put it
> on the bag-rack. Take your hat off!'
> 'What does that say on the signpost?
> "Harrogate" – where the beans come from?'
> 'No! That's Harro*coat*. Why don't you
> take your coat off? You could put it
> on the bag-rack. Don't you want to?
> It would only take a minute.
> Would you rather keep your coat on?
> Please yourself, then, keep your coat on.
> If you wanted, you could put it
> on the bag-rack. Take your coat off!...'

(The ms. becomes indecipherable at this point, apart from the few isolated fragments:

> ...cattle... splatter... in a blanket
> ...signal... goods train... on the down-line...)

Inter-City, lines 22/23, Kokur Niznegorsky: One of the more agreeable White Russians (more precisely, originating from Ukrainskaja SSR). See Johnson, ISBN 0 85533 002 3 (1971), p.200.

Clues

```
D
O         D
NOMDEPLUME
      X  P
         E
```

TOM O' BEDLAM'S BEAUTIES

(1981)

(I once considered nursing them
– even went for an interview
– magnanimous of me, eh?

Backed out – like them, eschewing
the risky Real for Illusion.)

?

Sired by *Surgical* *Sundries Inc.,*
my appearance – patent pending – is awesome.
I am not fettled from fleeces of thick wool,
no knitter's needles knocked me up.
Silkworms that dextrously adorn the sleek web
with *wyrda cræftum* couldn't make me;
yet, in institutions, internationally
men will attest me a tight-fitting raiment.

Say, supple-minded master of wit,
wealthy in words, what my name is.

Concord

*To transfer an outside call from your own
extension to another internal
extension: press the button on top of
your phone and dial the required extension;
when the dialled extension answers, replace
your receiver – leaving the outside call
in direct contact with the extension
to which you have transferred it. To obtain
an outside line, dial 9. Make sure every
call is absolutely necessary!*

Twenty years ago, the Sales Manager
(who was then a ledger-clerk) had a most
serious motor-cycle accident,
damaging the cranium and driving
certain bones of the left hip-joint into
the stomach; bouts of depression and crass
idiocy, an extravagant limp
and dyspepsia are the by no means
unnatural consequences. His is
extension 40 (on the 7th floor).

Motivated by insouciance, the
Despatch Clerk idly amuses himself
correcting the grosser solecisms
committed by his superiors to
print in the monthly house magazine (called
Info-Flo). He is particularly
distressed by certain excesses of the
Sales Manager's homespun Doric syntax.
The Sales Manager is unaware that
his company employs a Despatch Clerk.

The Despatch Clerk is unaware of the
Sales Manager's function, recognising
only the semi-literacy of
an author whose extension is 40.
Outraged and intent on retribution,
he dials 40 – replacing the phone as
soon as the Sales Manager yaps 'Sales Manager
speaking –' as the receiver is replaced.

In addition to those problems outlined
above, the Sales Manager has lately
been under stress (the Export Drive) at work,
has learned of the infidelity of
his wife (to a carpet-slipper salesman),
is pained by newly sprouted haemorrhoids
and is being pressed by one Manny Charles
(Turfster) over a debt in excess of
eight hundred pounds. The phone rings. An ulcer
twinges. 'Sales Manager here –' line goes dead.

Seventeen times during the afternoon.
the Despatch Clerk phones extension 40,
replacing the receiver as soon as
the Sales Manager answers (each answer
increasing in volume with each new call).
Between each call to the Sales Manager,
he dials 9 to obtain an outside line
and phones a number which happens to be
the ISBN of his latest book.
'*Concord Dry Cleaners*, Welshpool' (each answer

increasing in volume with each new call),
as the receiver is each time replaced.
On the instant that the 17th call
to Welshpool has been peevishly answered
('*Concord Dry Clean* – what's the game, you bastard?!'),
the Despatch Clerk presses the button on
top of his phone and dials extension four-
nought (which is answered immediately and
very irately indeed 'Sales bloody
Manager! What do you want, you shit-house?!'),

replacing his receiver – leaving the
outside call in direct contact with the
extension to which he has transferred it.

> ring ring ringingtone ring-a-ding-a-ding
> dialling tone a continuous purring
> ringing tone a repeated burr-burring
> engaged a repeated single note beeeee
> hello hello hello Sales Manager
> ha ha ha ha ha ha ha ha ha ha
> steady note number unobtainable

> equipment now ready for your nice call
> the number called or the post office lines
> are in use Sales Manager ha ha ha
> the nice equipment is trying to call
> the dialled number burr-burr-burr-burr-burr-burr
> the standard tones and their meanings are these
> Carpet Slippers the three-o-clock Haydock
> pass my crotchet repeat a single note
> please try again a few minutes later
> I never phoned the bloody dry cleaners

> ring ring ringingtone burr-burr-burr-burr-burr
> hello Sales Manager ha ha ha ha
> number eight hundred unobtainable
> please try again a few minutes later
> I never phoned the bloody dry cleaners
> where are you taking me ring-a-ding-dong
> burn my slippers and pile my crotcheter
> I never phoned the bloody dry cleaners
> piles try again a few minutes later

'Any change, Nurse?' 'No change, Doctor Snieder.'

Alma Mater

A rather solitary boy –
we were hardly aware of him until
one day, when we were in 5C,
in Assembly, as the Assistant Head
was intoning the Lord's Prayer, he sang

> *If you go down to the woods today*
> *You'd better not go alone,*
> *It's lovely down in the woods today*
> *But safer to stay at home*

loud and was removed during the second verse.

About a week later, in Chemistry,
Mr Watts discovered him writing up
his account of the preparation of
sodium thiosulphate crystals
in an unusual manner i.e.
he would do a few lines and then invert
his exercise book before scrawling
the next bit – alternate paragraphs
upside-down. When asked why, he replied
'In Japan the natives eat fish raw.'

Some days later, he seized Mr Hotchkiss
(a small History teacher) by the throat
crying 'At the roadside rooks snatch voles!'

About three-quarters of the way through
the Autumn Term, he left (I believe
to conclude his education elsewhere).

Hardfhip Aboard American Sloop The Peggy, 1765

Sailed for New York from Azores,
October 24th,
American floop the *Peggy*
(Mafter, Captain Harrifon),
cargo of wine and brandy
alfo a negro flave.

Storm blew up from North-Eaft,
rigging feverely damaged,
could make no way, d'ye fee?
Harrifon rationed all hands,
one pound of dry bread per day,
one pint of water and wine.

Hull fprung breach below water,
two veffels paffed – foul conditions
prevented communications,
rations reduced by degrees,
no food or water remained,
hands drunk on brandy and wine.

By December 25th
clement weather prevailed,
a fail was fpied, but its fkipper,
damn his eyes, ignored our fignal,
all hands pierced the air with fcreams
more pitiful than mews' wails.

Only liveftock aboard –
two pigeons and the fhip's cat,
doves flain for Chriftmas Dinner,
flew the cat two days later,
divided it into nine,
head was the Captain's portion.

After the cat, the negro.
Fell on his knees, begged mercy.
Dragged him into the fteerage,
fhot through the head by James Doud.
Kindled a fire abaft
to fry entrails and liver.

Mr James Campbell, half ftarved,
rufhed forward, ripped out the liver,
ftuffed it raw into his mouth.
The reft of us, after feafting,
pickled the body's remains –
threw head and fingers o'erboard.

James Campbell died raving mad
three days later, from eating
the liver raw. Fearing much,
left we all contract his madnefs,
refrained from eating Campbell,
caft body unto the fea.

By January 26th
the corpfe of the flave was ate.
Drew lots to fee who was next,
myfelf, David Flat, foremaft man,
felected the fhorteft ftraw,
afked to be defpatched quickly.

Reft of the hands decided
to wait till 11 o'clock
next day before flaying me
left deliverance fhould arrive.
That night my fenfes quit me –
'tis faid they have not returned.

At 10 a veffel hove-to,
the *Sufannah* bound for London
(Mafter, Thomas Evers),
took furvivors aboard,
myfelf in a fwoon, raving,
reached Land's End March 2nd.

To this day fometimes I fee them:
Captain David Harrifon,
James Doud, Lemuel Afhley,
James Warren, Samuel Wentworth,
eyes like a frightened horfe's
of the neger, whites uplifted.

Eclogue

A Range Rover stopped outside our door
    in a smug Shropshire village;
out steps our local Councillor,
    first-class shit.

'What we need is chaps like you
    to dig out the bodies
if there's a nucular' (sic) 'to-do,
    or bury the bodies –

there is no room for apathy
    even in our small village.'
'Sir, you reveal yourself to be
    a greater ass than we thought.

I know you for a parvenu,
    Vincent Greenback,
with a Used-Car Showroom or two –
    back to your roots.

Shrivelled in the Pentagon,
    Parochial Councillor,
squats the Cadaverous Thespian –
    may well undo us.

Go whimper in your reinforced
    fallout bunker,
if you are spared I'm happier lost,
    I'm old-fashioned.

I'll spade manure in my own trench.
    See these headlines?
THEATER KNOCKS OUT AUDIENCE;
    slays 'em all, slays 'em all.'

Tom o' Bedlam's Beauties *

In the summer hols we cycled
as far as the green water-tower
in the grounds of which grew apples.

Broken Bass bottles, embedded
in the cement-skimmed wall,
we bridged with tough hide school satchels.

Once within, we filched unripe
fruit – English old-fashioned names
like *Tom o' Bedlam's Beauties*.

The water-tower watchman, too,
had old-fashioned lingo – 'Grrr!
Young varmints!' – as in the *Beano*.

Returning, we munched apples under
another red brick buttressed wall.
Sated, we sought diversion.

Scaling a steep brick triangle,
peering over the parapet,
a prison-like scene was presented.

Close-cropped men in brown denim
tended a formal flower garden
behind which, a house with barred windows.

The nearest gardener glopped
but seemed not to see us, holding
his rake upside-down by the prongs.

Another solemnly knelt
chewing the bloom of a red
Hybrid Tea – *Ena Harkness*, I think.

* Old Herefordshire name for variety of eating-apple.

We pelted them with our cores
and all we could not consume.
Some of us scored direct hits.

The one with the upside-down rake
raised his palms to the sky
and visibly, audibly, wept.

Gigglingly biking back,
we resolved to repeat the prank
discreetly dubbed *Sanes and Loonies*.

Bereft

The only one left who could use a scythe
in all Onibury, or pleach a hedge
the *old* way: but could not understand
how the electric cooker worked or
(and this takes some believing) the light switched on –
when his wife died he sat in the dark, hungry.

Dialled the Surgery with my assistance,
held the phone in two paws like a sad dog
gnawing a bone, not knowing which end spoke.

Limns

'The coffee is free,'
an unctuous maître d'hôtel
once told him at lunch.
'If it's free it is ghastly,
or you, sir, are a jackass.'

*

There was no Party
capable of embracing
his oscillations
of extreme political
wrath. He never once voted.

*

In the SCR
of the new Polytechnic
he brooded aloof
estranged with the stuffy *Times*
amid *Guardian* hairies.

*

Loathing his best friends,
all he could muster at last
was a tolerant
indifference towards their
passionately held tenets.

*

His final words were
(directed to his best friend):
'No doubt as a child
you were starved, stunted with gin,
and suffered to get rickets.'

Wandering

Permit me to parley – Brigadier Peregrine
Fashpoint-Shellingem (author of *Peruvian
Jungle by Kayak, With a Kodak in Kooju,
Huskies Away!, Hottentots Were My Neighbours,
In the Bush with the Blacks of Booloo-Kishooloo,*
&c. &c. &c. &c.),
K.C.B., M.V.O., F.R.G.S.

                    Oh, I
know that I probably don't seem the type, as we
prune back this gnarled Hybrid Tea *Ena Harkness* and
rake the first leaves from the lawns to the compost heaps
tucked in triangular shadows of buttresses
(daily, the sun getting lower, the wall higher),
but, I assure you, the world *was* my whatsaname
(damn funny thing; can't remember the word for it).

Camped with the Indians, pure Tehuelche blood,
on the bleak plateaux of cold Patagonia,
cattle crashed down under bowled bolladores there –
feet drawn together noosed, tail stuck up rigidly.

Saw summers on the Salween when the river rose
fifty feet overnight flinging up cottage-sized
boulders like pitched pebbles, porters splashed into pulp.

Camped at the edge of the East Rongbuk Glacier,
gale reached its maximum, 1 a.m. 26th,
wild flapping canvas made noise like machine-gun fire,
fine frozen spindrift thrashed into our sleeping-bags.
Jettisoning empty oxygen-cylinders,
each clanged like church-bell rings into the East Rongbuk.

Fell through the floes with a dog-team in Labrador,
slashed free the harnesses, swam for the nearest ice,
stripped off my garments and beat the freeze out of 'em,
still couldn't last the night, had to kill all the dogs,
skinned 'em and made a rough coat with the hair inside,
piled up the dead bodies, cuddled up close to 'em,
lasted till morning, relief-ship arrived, by Gad.

Plied down the Pyrene River in wild Peru,
Indian, Quinchori, built twenty rafts for us,
bartered with five rolls of cloth, knives and ornaments,
balsa logs pinned with hard splinters of chonta wood,
spray flew on all sides up, rainbowing rays of sun...

Sometimes it seems a long, long while ago to me...
all I can do to remember events when that
damnation Matron, whatever her name is, says
'Now then, of *course* you're a brave, brave explorer man.
Tell Doctor' (whatsisname) 'Snyderson all about
nice Patagonia, *"Brigadier"* Peregrine.'

Four Poems *

Love warps the mind a little from the right.
CRABBE

I

A leather thong round your neck,
a silver band round your right wrist;
these and a mouthful of sweetness,
Chyorniye Glaza (Black Eyes),
I think of as you are removed from me
'For your own safety, you understand?'

II

From the superior height of omnibus
two may be seen through the sunshine-roof
of their tiny cerulean Citroën
fondly mutually massaging genitals
(lump under blue denim, mound under black cord).

Love, still persisted in, has not kept pace
with the rest of evolution – lights change,
gears mesh, all hurtle towards the river,
except these, oblivious, stalled in the Slow Lane.

III

His left hand cups, gently lifts a plump boob,
applies soft pressures. A pool on the platform,
where orfe swim under the twin white faces,
mirrors the guilt and gilt, and concentric
circles widen as shock-waves approach –
an unseen locomotive is going
to uncouple even these most loving.

* from the Russian of Kokur Niznegorsky

186

IV

Silvaner Feodosiisky
had the Tsarina's handmaid
in the State Bathroom – her bum
bare on a cold marble slab
adjacent the basin, her legs
wide-splayed, he standing up straight;
behind them an opulent gilt
mirror recorded their native
ups and downs. What could be lusher?
– Naught, *since those days*, Mother Russia!

Interior

Lady in blue dungarees
(once garment of honest tradesmen)
extremely intense indeed –
'Michael, I worry about you.
How do you *really relax?*'
'Having my hair cut is restful.'
Ford Worker builds, in his spare time,
immovable vast concrete boat –
announces it is an Art Form.
'Are you *really* re*lax*ing now?'
This writer has never tackled
a single *major* issue.
(Was unaware there were any.)
Incomprehensible Ulsterman
opinionates on some author –
one 'Liam o'Reece', to my ears.
The scissors are plying (restfully).
I confess ignorance of this
Hibernian homme de lettres.
(Outrage) 'Ye *must* have heard of him!
He wrote the bestseller *Exodus!*'
They are worried about calandrias
and Grigorievich Grigorenko.

Unassailed by such anxieties,
perhaps I should retrain to program
dumb Artificial Intelligence
in unmeasured no bullshit language –
ALGOL and COBOL and FORTRAN.

Artemus' Wardrobe

Gents Owtfitters, now, hold me in grate or,
becuz the following befell me wunce.

Requiring britches and a dressing-gown,
I haysund to the neyburhood Booteek
and did not find it difficult to chuze
garments appropriate to my fizzeek.
The Chaingin Room wuz fitted with a daw
sitch as Salunes have in a Wild West town –
opening both ways, maid of slats of wood,
exposing heds an neez but not full-frunce.
I dond the Paisley robe with greater plum
and vood the mirrer with a grate enthoos.
But, hitchin up the trowzerz, as I stood
balansin on wun legg, I nearly cumm
a cropper – hopt ter save meself, an lent
on the accursid daw. It throo me owt.
I hopt a pays ore too, wylst givin vent
too me emowshunz, & herd someone showt
'A Bedlamite, got luce without is droors!' –
the most embarrassust I ever bean.
The ground flew up and hit me on all fores.
I girdid up my Lions & fled the Seen.

Visit

Façade, a peeling Georgian.
Lake (Capability Brown),
drained – for obvious reasons.
In the Orangery, quiet men in smocks
lift dull malevolent eyes
(Art can help; so can Drama).
West Wing, converted to quarters
where one jabbers into a phone
devoid of connecting wire
(A great deal of patience is needed).
Eleventh-century Dovecote,
remodelled for Thespian therapy.
Subhuman screech from the woodwork-shop
judders dust motes in the cool
Private Chapel, a nave
flooded ultramarine,
MVCH+LOVED+HVSBAND+AND+FATHER
IN+HIS+THIRTY+SECOND+YEAR
WITHOVT+COMMAND+OF+HIS+FACVLTIES.

Amulet

The image of Christophorus,
to mid-calf in the flood
with hitched-up skirt, convincing
weight entrusting to staff,
the nipper on his shoulder
smugly raising two fingers,
owes much to Dierick Bouts
(mid-15th cent., Low Countries),
but reduced, incised in silver
on a tiny disc round her neck
at which you stare from three inches
whilst snorting in copulation.

> She is waxy and pale yellow,
> hard to manipulate,
> stiff fingers clutch at a charm.
> Ambulance, panda car, press.
> 'She must have been desperate! Christ!...
> Oh Christ! If my wife finds out...'
> *But you do not know this yet;*
> *it happens eight hours from now.*

She snuggles into your shoulder
sobbing and falls asleep deeply.
She has taken fifty or more,
but you do not know this. You know
that the amulet owes much
to Bouts's Christophorus.

Some of Their Efforts *

I

All here suffer Modern Maladies:

Jet Lag, Road Signs in Welsh,
Dyslexia, Anorexia,
Child Imbecility brought about by
Spaghetti Junction petrol fumes,
The Petrol Shortage, Nasty Ulsters
(real kind cannot spare
very much humanity),
L'amor che muove
il sole e Black Holes,
Writer's Block, Spondee/Trochee/Dactyl
(sounds of damp, lumbering, obsolete fauna).

II

How unnerving to meet Dr Schynieder
& his burly white-coated apprentice
with his Jungian remarks
& a skull-cap that sparks
& a stiff reinforced canvas jacket
& a plaque ready-labelled HIC+IACET
PEREGRINVS+NON+COMPOS+MENTIS.

How diverting to see one's companions
involuntarily flex their thighs
as their wires are plugged in
with a matronly grin
by Nurse who manipulates wails
as a virtuoso scales
in a two finger exercise.

* See Glibber & Crass, 'Therapeutic value of Poetry practised amongst the mentally disturbed,' Feb. 1979, *Transact. Soc. Cephalic Research*, p. 119. For the strong tendency in our nearest allies, the monkeys, in microcephalous idiots, and in the barbarous races of mankind, to imitate whatever they hear, see Vogt, *'Mémoire sur les Microcéphales,'* 1867, p. 169.

III

Natives are nice, they call me 'Bwana',
only their lingo is loco – they call
the Belgian Congo 'Ward 17B'.
Last night I fought a croc underwater;
Medicine-Man said it was a 'Mattress'.
In this jungle coons wear white linen coats.
Shhh! There ventures the wily okapi.
I have perfected swinging on creepers,
slow-motion grandfather-clock pendulum
over the canyon bosky with palm fronds,
creamy the foaming creek, the water-hole
harbouring hippopotami. Pygmies
are awe-struck at my *Aaoo-aaoo-aas!*
Chimps are my chums. Jane wears cheetah-skin bras.

IV

Weissmuller wakes us nightly with a shriek,
beating his wizened dugs like bongo-drums,
simian brain in simian physique.

A scratched LP *Symphonie Fantastique*
is therapeutic – *Dies Irae* thrums,
Weissmuller wakes us nightly with a shriek.

Rain on the Art Class window pelts oblique,
Van Gogh receives undue encomiums –
simian brain in simian physique.

Nurses dance with us; waltz-time, cheek-to-cheek,
Weissmuller lets his hand stray to their bums
(Weissmuller wakes us nightly). With a shriek,

Matron repels an amatory tweak –
he says 'You Jane, me Tarzan. Let's be chums!'
Simian brain in simian physique

was once *outside* the brick wall with that clique
of fortunates. Another autumn comes,
Weissmuller wakes us nightly with a shriek,
simian brain in simian physique.

Extruding absentmindedly remorse
incalculable providential croon
reflect resourceful Japanese fish course
interminable efflorescent spoon;
landed excruciating gentry meant
intestinal unease – th' Olympic Champ.
Wherefore go jovial unto thy tent
wherein, betimes, walls wax exceeding damp.

Nevertheless, Concord with Hybrid Tea
conspires withal, crass Patagonian
Sales Managers are here and so are we.
Up, Jenkins, heretofore Etonian,
grid up your lioness, escaler wall!
Thrall! Thrall, rapscallion! Thrall! Thrall! Thrall! Thrall!

Ornithological Petrarchan

> *It is difficult to portray bird voices in writing, because birds*
> *rarely make 'human' sounds, and our interpretations vary: one*
> *person hears a call-note as 'teu', another as 'chew' or 'sioo'.*
>
> PETERSON, MOUNTFORT & HOLLOM,
> *A Field Guide to the Birds of Britain and Europe* (Collins)

Calidris maritima pipes *'weak wit'*,
Gypaetus barbatus thinly cries *'queer'*,
the Pheasant's *'cork cock'* oft' delights the ear,
the Little Stint, when flushed, has a sharp *'tit'*,
Calidris alba calls on us to *'quit'*,
the Reed Bunting's alarm call *'shit'* rings clear.
Is this *Calidris canutus* we hear?
Hark! a low *'nut'*, in flight, a whistling *'twit'*.

But what is this deep sighing *'oo-oo-oo'*
more moaning than *Strix aluco*? *'Quick quick!'*
Turnix sylvatica's *'croo croo crooo CROOO'*
bursts from a bush. A hard explosive *'prik'*
(from *Coccothraustes coccothraustes)* sends
exciting vibes to sensitive nerve-ends.

Phrenfy

The Mafter's phrenfy having continued long,
his left eye fwelled unto an hen's egg fize
fo that the furgeon daily feared 'twould burft.

Th' extreme pain of this tumour caufed the Mafter
to be awake a month. On fome occafion
it took four other perfons and myfelf
to hold him in reftraint 'gainft his defire
to tear his own eye out with his own hands.

Thence he continued filent one whole year.
In this ftate of poor helplefs idiocy
he languifhed.

On November 30th
I went into his chamber – 'twas his birthday,
and bonfires and illuminations marked
th' refpect the townffolk felt at the event.
I fpoke to him about thefe preparations
to which he faid 'All folly, Mrs Ridgeway.
They had done better letting it alone.'

A few months afterwards, on my removing
a fharp knife from his grafp, he faid 'I am
that which I am, I am that which I am'
and in fix minutes, poor fad fimpleton,
whifpered the fame thing two or three times more.

One day, calling his fervant to his fide
but being quite unable to exprefs
any defires, he fhewed figns of diftrefs
and great uneafinefs and faid at length
'I am a fool'. On fome occafion later,
his fervant having taken away his watch,
he called the menial and faid 'Bring it here'.

His laft words, fpoken to his fervant when
that gentleman was breaking a large hard coal,
were 'That is a ftone, you blockhead'. He was quiet
a twelvemonth afterwards and died in filence.

About How Many?

About one in six.
What kind of people?
People like us.
Who hasn't wanted
to scream the house down?
Felt there was no point
carrying on?
Sat day-dreaming
at place of employment?
Wouldn't be human
if you hadn't.
Why do five million
people per annum
visit their doctor?...
More working days lost
than flu and bad backs.
All walks of life –
executives, soldiers,
old-age pensioners
(hommes de lettres?).
'Different'? 'Odd'?
Require reassurance.
Occupational
and industrial
therapy units
help, as can Fine Art,
Music and Drama.
Tolerance, patience,
talk freely to them,
build warm relaxed
relationships with them.

65th

1916: Yehudi Menuhin
and you, thank God, were born. Be, when you in-
dulge in your birthday dram, aware of this:
to whippersnappers like me you're *not* his-
tory, but *present*, learnt by heart in bits
to keep us sane whilst dealing with the shits
daily we've the misfortune to confront
(at work there's one particular such cunt,
Company Secretary, tick of ticks,
advocates closing Tate re Fire Bricks)
and to remind us that, as well as bruising,
poems, and life, can also be amusing
and dignified and common-sensed and sexy
and much more fun and certainly more flexi-
ble than they seemed before.

                         .Congratulations!
Jolly good show! Chin chin! Cheers! Jubilations!
Here's to all Ewart's and (nunc est bibendum!)
Melpomene and Thalia who blend 'em.

The Euphemisms

Crackers, Potty, Loony, Bonkers,
Nutty, Screwy, Ga-Ga, Dull,
Strange, Do-Lally, Dopey, Silly,
Touched, A Bit M., Up the Pole,

Zany, Crazy, Dotty, Batty,
Round the Bend, Remedial, Slow,
Cranky, Turned, Moonstruck, Quixotic,
Odd, Beside Oneself, Loco,

Rambling, Giddy, Flighty, Crackbrained,
Soft, Bewildered, Off One's Head,
Wandering, Wild, Bereft of Reason,
Daft, Distracted, Unhingèd;

attributes of Simple Simons,
Asses, Owls, Donkeys, Mules,
Nincompoops, Wiseacres, Boobies,
Noodles, Numskulls, Gawks, Tomfools,

Addle/Silly/Chuckle/Dunder/
Sap/Bone/Block/Thick/Muddle/Crack-
Heads, The E.S.N., The Balmy,
Silly Billies, Dunces, Jack-

Asses, Dullards, Merry Andrews,
Mooncalves, at least one MP,
Vauxhall·Workers (and Execs), Clods,
Paisleyites, Twerps, Plaid Cymru...

Tanka *

'That's very tiny,'
she says (probes his kimono);
icy December,
the *Rose* shut, she ugly – what's
expected, the HINDENBURG?

* After Sanraku Koshu

Between the Lines

VERDICT RETURNED ON EX SALES EXECUTIVE...
MISSING FROM 'BAY TREES' MENTAL HOSPITAL...
TOOK OWN LIFE WHILE BALANCE OF MIND...

*

Strange headaches, following a road accident, caused me, in adolescence, to attempt suicide by the following interesting method.

I lived in Crewe. One night, intoxicated from the Station Hotel and further provided for with a half-bottle of cheap brandy in my duffle-coat pocket, I scaled a barrier of vertically erected sleepers, thereby gaining access to the railway. Perhaps twenty different lines to choose from, white in the full moon and frost, like a mesh of elephant tusks. The rails I selected met at infinity, then widened again, criss-crossed together and apart like windscreen-wipers (this distressing effect I attribute to drink). Uncorking the Cognac, I settled supine on a sleeper – heels resting on one rail, neck neatly flat on the other, throat up to the stars. The spirit was coarse, like raw mustard on the nasal tissues, but was drained in five minutes. I regained consciousness in exactly the same position, throat across the line, at nine o'clock on the following morning. Tangles of last season's groundsel and willow-herb entwined long-rusty unused track where I lay cold. 3 feet away the 0859 to Cardiff (via Shrewsbury) gathered speed on an adjacent track.

*

MEDIC CLAIMS PRESSURE OF BUSINESS CAUSED BREAKDOWN...
SUICIDE-RATE SOARS FOR INDUSTRY CHIEFS...
TOP EXECS FIND IT TOO TOUGH AT THE TOP...

*

Climbed the wall by the red brick buttress, broken glass on the parapet drew blood. Limped through moonlit quiet fields. Dogs' howls and klaxon fading after the first mile waist-deep in cold fen-water. Suddenly breaking cover to wood-smoke and light from a tinker's caravan camped in a sunk lane, hawthorn hedge splodged with drying linen – red green and blue parakeets perched fluttering pierced on white may, and beyond, in the moon, bright steel cusp of railway lines gleaming...

199

A Departure

Susurration of rushes,
deck-chair poised at the weir edge,
strepitumque Avon avari.
Valetudinarian gent,
kitted as for a safari
in pith helmet and white ducks,
has sat unmoving for four hours.
A cleg enters him by the nose.

Evening; chromatic thrushes,
territorial blackbirds' clucks,
purring from fumous wallflowers
and lilac, discordantly rent.
St John's men raise him from dank sedge,
stiff, still in a sitting pose.

Legacies

I once inherited a parcel of port from the cellar of an old friend.

I walked the two miles from the station to his house in silver February sunshine. The gravel of the long driveway crackled underfoot.

I had arranged with National Wine Carriers Ltd that the cases, a dozen or so, should be collected that day, and, after briefly exchanging greetings with my old army pal's widow, Ethel Fashpoint-Shellingem, I hastened to the cellar, where, by the light of a candle, I applied myself to the pleasurable task of gently removing the old bottles from their bins and crating them in straw for their journey to my own cellars.

When the last of the cases was carefully nailed shut, I proceeded to transfer them one by one up the hollowed stone steps into the hallway to await the arrival of the van.

As I was crossing the thickly carpeted reception room with the last case (a dozen of Noval 'Nacional' '63 – a sort of 'modern pre-phylloxera' from ungrafted vines, truly magnificent wine, still await-ing its prime in my bins now, toughness softening, fruit beginning to show beautifully as the spirit integrates...), an odd noise from the top of the broad oak staircase caused me to pause.

A noise such as one might use to instruct a horse to accelerate, only higher in pitch – 'Gerrupp-upp-upp' – wafted down from the master bedroom followed by uncontrolled hysterical sobbing followed by 'I simply, gerrupp-upp-upp, can't go on-nn, ho-ho-o-o, God hel-l-p me-e-e'.

I hurriedly added the case of 'Nacional' to the others, then evasively slipped out of the front door and down the gravel.

'Peregrine's popping off like that must have upset the old bird, I suppose,' I supposed to myself. 'Still, better pull yourself together, Ethel old girl, or you'll end up like poor Perry – finish your days in the Bin.'

At the main gate I met the little chap in the NWC van.

'I say,' I said, 'go easy with those cases o'man – somewhere in that lot there's a dozen of '27 Taylors (absolutely superb balance and wonderfully long finish, you know) and half a dozen 1857s of an unknown shipper (probably starting to fade a bit now in fruit and sweetness, becoming rather dry and spirituous, and the colour pale amber by now, I shouldn't be at all surprised).'

Testimoliums

'Will it mend busted telephones?'
'Have we had testimoliums? Oh we've had testimoliums all right.'
(EAVESDROPPED)

'The egg-cup was a proper mess
after my Alfred threw it in
the fire. But FIXO done it up.'

       'It's *super* stuff for mending bust
       Airfix Fokker triplane struts!'
       Says Jason Ashley (12) of Esher.

'Didn't know which way to turn
when Auntie's vase got broke. But thanks
to FIXO it's as good as new.'

       'When I want satisfaction, I
       get FIXO. FIXO every time!'
       MacDonald (Mrs), Aberdeen.

Colonel Fashpoint-Shellingem
(retired) of Cheltenham Spa, reports:
'Damn good for gluin fishin-rods.'

       'This pot is cracked, I am afraid.
       If anything *can* patch it up
       it's FIXO. And if FIXO can't
       then *nothing* can – you mark my words.'

There seem to be so many of them,

not only the mildly amusing
(the man I meet in a Mexico
City urinal, kilted,
convinced he is Robert the Bruce;
the old bird in Paddington Buffet,
whom we studiously try to ignore,
singing the following ditty
to the tune of *Rosin the Bow*
in coyote-like contralto:

> *I'm Queen Nizzagooloo the mighty*
> *Adored by the moon and the stars*
> *Abooloo abooloo abighty*
> *Nimooloo nimooloo nimars...)*

but also the awfully frightening
(the bloke next door used to wake us
at 3 o'clock every morning
bellowing things like 'Out, hounds!
Vile spawn of Beelzebub!
The Police are Capitalist Puppets!'
He would often run into the garden
and joust with the rhododendrons.
He once threw a wardrobe downstairs
screaming 'So much for Goethe's *Faust!*'
In the early hours of the morning
before he was hospitalised
his shouts were attended by scrawks
from his small children and his wife
and a subsequent slamming of front door
and a sobbing and running of feet.
In the daylight, a trail of dark red,
in blobs every two or three inches,
led all the way up the street
to the Cottage Hospital portals.).

And the reasons are legion. They vary
from inherited duff chromosomes
to car-crash damage and breakdowns
that you get from too much Exam-Cram.
And some quacks, I read, blame our diets –
some brain cells, it seems, are allergic
to some foods (I once ate a haggis
and felt strange for several days).

And if none of these claims us, appalling
age, like a fuddling narcotic,
has the same effect on the rest of us.

Song of the Bedsit Girl

I'm frozen in amber by street-light,
        pine-wallpaper planks box me in,
the phial on the faded mat opens
        an alternative to the Bin.

I shouldn't have left my husband
        if the *other man* hadn't occurred –
told me he loved me more than his wife,
        the turd.

At first I just wanted to screw him
        that night in the Tudor Rose.
Now I'm helpless and hollow and rue him
        when, after coming, he goes.

Now the sheets are brown-stained and arctic,
        oh! love's a perfidious fink,
and I snuffle the bed like a truffle-pig
        desperate to retrace his stink.

Now my head is filling with feathers,
    my thumb gnawed down to the quick,
all for true love of a man him*self*
        (not just a prick).

CHORUS:

Don't fall for charisma or intellect,
    your motives were better venereal –
your men in the Arts are bastards and farts
    to whom love is mere raw material.

Ariadne deserted by Theseus
    had heartaches enough when you tally 'em,
but at least Dionysus helped her through her crisis –
    our victim has only Valium.

& the thumb bones crunch & the knot-holes howl
    & my head is filling with amber
& a truffle-pig in a feather wig
    plays a stone viola da gamba

& the tune is He Loves Me/He Loves Me Not
    & the empty phial rasps on the mat
& the stained sheets are cold & the tears are hot
    oh! My Darling/My Fucking Rat!

Commitment

'Tom's in a "Rest Home" under Doctor Snyde.
Gerald's so nice, a carpet-slipper rep, –
he fell head-over-heels for me – I pride
myself on my appearance (it's a step
up in the world to ride round in a Merc.).
About the time of my *affaire* with Gerry,
Tom went right off the rails ("Pressure of Work"
the Doctor said; he certainly went very
odd – once, when he came home from the office,
he smashed the phone up, shouting "ring-a-ding"
and "burr-burr-burr", then sat, drinking black coffees,
all night), Pressure of Work's a funny thing.
His raving yells, his sobbing and his quarrels
obliged us to commit him to "The Laurels".'

?

Can you guess me? A garment; not knitted, though, nor ornate,
not slinky skin-tight silk nor stretched-transparent tulle,
neither the pelt of the whale nor white North Pole bear.
Royal violet velvet, poxed office-clerks' poplin;
composed of neither of these am I. Classless;
vassal, my stiff canvas fits tight, or viscount.

Without my weave, un-wise would wave their arms weirdly.

NOTES

?: see final note.

Artemus' Wardrobe: W.P.C. Elliott is quoted in the *Cheltenham Chronicle* of December 17th 1973 as stating,

> On April 2nd 1973, on duty outside His 'n' Hers Boutique, a sound of voices raised drew my attention, investigating which I found a man (clad in a Paisley dressing-gown, his trousers dangling round his ankles thus exposing his private parts) leaping into the air on one leg while a crowd looked on and applauded. On seeing me he fled and I gave chase, detaining him at last in Lingerie. He gave his name as one Charles Farrar Browne (born 1834 in Maine, New England), resident of Les Lauriers Nursing Home.

Some of Their Efforts: 'Natives are nice...' and the Villanelle – the following was abstracted from a copy of the *Telegraph* of April 27th 1979.

> Former Olympic swimmer and Tarzan star Johnny Weissmuller was transferred yesterday from a home for retired actors to a mental hospital after complaints that the 75-year-old ex-champ was disturbing other residents with his 'chest-beating' and 'Tarzan-calls' in the early hours of the morning.

Some of Their Efforts: the terminal sonnet 'Extruding absent-mindedly remorse...' – cf. 'Alma Mater' (p.177), the hero's account of the preparation of sodium thiosulphate crystals; cf. also Gavin Ewart, 'Two Nonsense Limericks' (p. 33, *All My Little Ones*, Anvil Press in association with Rex Collings, 1978); cf. also 'Sonnet found in a Deserted Mad-House', Anon. (p. 227, *Penguin Book of Comic and Curious Verse*, selected by J.M. Cohen, 1952).

?: cf. Riddle 35, *The Exeter Book*, Part II, edited by W.S. Mackie (Oxford, 1933).

DIPLOPIC

(1983)

Optician, I am having Double Visions
to see one thing from two sides. Only
give me a Spectacle and I am delighted.

ENGLISH PHRASES FOR MALAY VISITORS
(Vest-Pocket Editions, 1950)

*

(1) Vulture, aloof on a thermal;
frail flesh is a commodity
to be scavenged.
(2) Vulture, manipulating still-bloody bones
on the white sand;
Poet, ordering the words of a beautiful sonnet
on the bare page.

TWO VISIONS
(after Kokur Niznegorsky)

*

Is this Thalia and Melpomene, or am I seein double?

EAVESDROPPED
(in a Greek restaurant)

At Marsden Bay

Arid hot desert stretched here in the early
Permian Period – sand dune fossils
are pressed to a brownish bottom stratum.
A tropical saline ocean next silted
calcium and magnesium carbonates
over this bed, forming rough Magnesian
Limestone cliffs on the ledges of which
Rissa tridactyla colonises –
an estimated four thousand pairs
that shuttle like close-packed tracer bullets
against dark sky between nests and North Sea.
The call is a shrill 'kit-e-wayke, kit-e-wayke',
also a low 'uk-uk-uk' and a plaintive
'ee-e-e-eeh, ee-e-e-eeh'.

Four boys about sixteen years old appear
in Army Stores combat jackets, one wearing
a balaclava with long narrow eye-slit
(such as a rapist might find advantageous),
bleached denims rolled up to mid-calf, tall laced boots
with bright polished toe-caps, pates cropped to stubble.
Three of the four are cross-eyed, all are acned.
Communication consists of bellowing
simian ululations between
each other at only a few inches range:
'Gibbo, gerrofforal getcher yaffuga',
also a low 'lookadembastabirdsmon'.

Gibbo grubs up a Magnesian Limestone
chunk and assails the ledges at random,
biffing an incubating kittiwake
full in the sternum – an audible slap.
Wings bent the wrong way, it thumps at the cliffbase,
twitching, half closing an eye. Gibbo seizes
a black webbed foot and swings the lump joyously
round and round his head. It emits
a strange wheezing noise. Gibbo's pustular pal
is smacked in the face by the flung poultry, yowls,
and lobs it out into the foam. The four

gambol euphoric like drunk chimps through rock pools.
Nests are dislodged, brown-blotched shells crepitate
exuding thick rich orange embryo goo
under a hail of hurled fossilised desert
two hundred and eighty million years old.

Editorial

Being both *Uncle Chummy's Letter Box*
of *Kiddies' Column* and *Supa Scoop* besides
(*Your Headlines As They Happen*), and having the shakes
uncellophaning fags this crapulous morning,
I compose: BOY (13) CLUBS DAD TO DEATH,
CHILD (10) SCALDS GRANNY (87) TO DEATH,
SKINHEAD (14) STONES KITTIWAKES TO DEATH
AS RSPCA ASKS 'WHERE'S THE SENSE?'

Better this afternoon after the Vaults,
I award 50 pence to Adam (9)
for this: 'Dear Uncle Chummy, I am writing
to let you know about my hamster Charlie
who's my best friend...' 'Keep up the good work, kiddies...'
(sinister dwarfs, next issue's parricides).

Dark Continent

Big fat essays are being inserted
into resistant pigeon-holes. Chalky,
who once lived in Africa, is giving
the SCR the benefit of
his experience in those parts 'The *Nkonga
Herald* often carried reports
of offences of Chicken Buggery...'

Flora Mackenzie (2nd Year English)
has tackled, for her Creative Writing,
the sanguinary 'Death of a Grouse'
*(In crumpled feather wings of prayer
Heather she lived in, no man harming
She lies and bleeds her rose red root
Her wattle wilted willed to waste
The bird is free, man's lust is caged...*
etcetera, etcetera; God).

'The Prof's in a bit of a sweat. It seems
he picked up the Departmental Phone
and who should be on the other end
but Mrs Mackenzie – gave him pure Hell,
said Flora's run off with a 3rd Year Mining
Engineering student, a black,
one Bongoman Bulawayo, I think,
to Zimbabwe or somewhere, and she said
"Hoots! Toots! What are ye goin to do, mon?"
Prof said "Your daughter *is* over eighteen."
Well, she flew off the handle, said "Hoots! Toots!
I gave her to you in good faith..." '

                        A rose
finger of dawn caresses a mud hut,
awakens the delicate, shy, pale Flora
(who strains and frets under sleek black thew)
to that Dark Continent, where men
are men, and the poultry is very uneasy.

Receipt

Unto the stock, that hath been simmering
slowly for nearly twenty-four hours already,
cast ye a bushel of the following, mixed:
shoots of the sacred Ashphodeliaboo,
Roogin, Wormwillow, Auberjelly Lime,
Elephant Quince, Sweet Portalooforago,
Smiley Potatoes, Voodoo Saxifrapple,
verdant Aspariagora, Zulu Froom,
Lily of fragrant Umpo, Virgin's Ice,
a stick of Popgo (black), two sprigs of Kak-Kak.
Marinade dugs, sliced thickly into steaks,
with Shamilee and crushed dried seeds of Xeppit
    (which method served to cook the white poetess
    Flora, 9th wife of the gourmand Bongoman).

The Terrestrial Globe

Señor García
descends a staircase
hopping on one hand.
Three steps down,
not unnaturally,
he sprains his wrist
and sprawls in the sawdust.
He leaps to his feet,
bows, bursts into tears.

Il Maestro subdues
two lionesses,
two Bengal tigresses
and one unidentified
heavily moulting
very male quadruped.

The Brothers Alfonso
perform on stilts.
One of them bears
a striking likeness
to *Señor García*
and, trying to do
'The very difficult
Backward Somersault',
falls on his head.
He removes his stilts,
bows, bursts into tears.

'And now, all the way
from West Germany'
(a bald Chinese
of ferocious aspect
and droopy moustaches
flexes her biceps),
'The Strongest Woman
The World Has Known,
Miss Herculess,
will carry *Miss Jill*
in this gigantic
Terrestrial Globe.'
Miss Jill climbs into
the ferrous contraption,
sealed in tight
with a saucer-like lid.
The Chinese raises
the huge sphere until
it is over her head
then hurls it clanging
into the ground.
The audience gasps,
screams come from within.
Anxious hands drag
Miss Jill out to safety,
blood smears her costume.
Miss Herculess shrieks,
first in Cantonese,
then in thick Glaswegian,
'D'ye ken I'm no blind!
Keep awa frae my mon!'

A dromedary
of prodigious age
is chased by two llamas
gratuitously
round several dozen
laps of the Big Top...

The Big Cats

                bicker. Fodens churn the rec
into an Auerbach slough. A squat grey bomb
of Calor hisses under a caravan
labelled not only JILL – CONTORTIONIST

but also SEÑOR GARCÍA – FABULOUS
MANIPULATOR EXTRAORDINAIRE
and also THE STRONGEST WOMAN KNOWN TO MAN.
Two tigresses tease red skin, suck stiff bone.

Grunts, lately of the jungle, fade to moans.
The lettered van jolts on its springs. Pink bare
meat rises slowly in the steamed-up glass.
Glut, guzzle, slurp, drool, slobber, mumble, snort –

rank felines, scarcely tame, extravasate,
vie to possess inflamed raw purple flesh.

Minima

After

the telegram-boy's purse-lipped dirge,
the slicing open,
the ghastly revelation,

the bereaved Parnassian
hones a canine tooth,
sharpens a pencil.

Epicedium

Ah well, it could be worse – it could be *me*.

Telecommunication

The telegram-boy's little red Suzuki.
The pasted strips TELEPHONE FATHER URGENT.
The feeling trembly, squittery and pukey.
The breakfast things left in the cold detergent.
The milled edge of a coin on the thumb-pad.
The voice at the other end 'Yes, late last night'.
The feeling scared/exhilarated/numb. Sad
memories of – (enough of all that shite) .

The puny hug, meant to propitiate.
Strong, palliating Fino de Jerez.
The weak reply, meant to initiate
a five-year-old into peculiar Death
'Yes, Grandma's bones *might* fossilise, of course,
like those in your *First Book of Dinosaurs.*'

War Artistes

*There is one of them War Artistes with our lot. He seems not
quite human. He drawers even when the heavy firing is on.
He done a water colours picture of poor Carew with his head
blowed clean off – a very pretty thing, and I don't think!
I think he SEES things different to us.*

From a letter to his brother, *c.* 1917, by Thomas Gibb,
in the author's possession.

We are always out there
   with pencils raised,
treacherous bastards,
   Double Agents
not working for *you*
   but for some Secret Power.

If an awful thing happens,
   we will appear –
coyotes, dingoes,
   jackals, hyenas,
lapping up
   universal holocausts.

We have a horrible
   kind of diplopia –
(1) straight, clinical,
   accurate, X-ray,
(2) refracted
   to serve our bent calling.

Mnemonics

Some matter is too delicate to define
with muted chalks or the restricted palette
implicit in small portable tubes of gouache
(e.g. the whitish-tallows and wax-yellows
and algal-greens of military flesh).
Mnemonics are essential – the best method
is to annotate draft studies in the field
for later more urbane studio finish.

May in the squares is the white of Devon cream,
in the warm sun ripe Georgian brick assumes
the russet of port half a century old.
Ribs bright cream, whitest teeth…wrote Kennington
on his Dead Jerry (*circa* 1916)
that hangs now in peaceful Clifford Street, West One.

P. S.

The stitching new on your tiny rectangle of black,
you immerse yourself in the sad therapy of the kitchen,
withdrawing from sight when assailed by trembling and weeping.
I mailed you my useless sympathy but, reticently,
withheld admiration and love for you (old-fashioned words)
who, having a grim chore to finish, get on with the job.

Hints

Find ways to make the narrative compel,
I advise students; as, in retailing this,
you might lend the issue added poignancy
by being distanced – describe the electrified
overgrown line in cool botanical terms,
white cow-parsley, *Anthriscus sylvestris*,
adding the child with anthropological
detachment, ten years old, print dress, bewildered...

Compelling, maybe, but mere narrative –
no moral or intellectual envoy.
Accentuate the dignified resilience
that humans, or some, are capable of still,
evinced in the sad braveness of the bereaved
whose daughter, being blind, observed no warning.

At Home

She is nearly 87,
and her house is ten years older.
In the garden huge old beech trees,
silver-boled in winter sunshine,
have the following carved on them
(though the scars are mossed and healed now):
JOHN CAREW L SALLY HIBBERT.
In her chair of woven basket,
in the window-bay with pot-plants,
she drinks Earl Grey every morning,
reads the *Telegraph* and wonders
why young people now are vicious,
disrespectful, stoned and randy.
On her knees a tartan blanket,
in her lap soft-centre bon-bons.
(An interior like that in
Lamb's *Portrait of Lytton Strachey*.)

In a silver cage a mynah
chews a grape and spits the pips out.
In a silver frame a photo
of a young World War I soldier
signed JC in faded sepia.

Carved black elephants, brass kettles
fitted with bright amber handles,
Taj Mahals by moonlight rendered
in bright dyes on thin silk, jewel-
hilted daggers indicate some
past connection with the Raj. Dates
gleam in chevrons down a central
spine in a round-ended carton.

*

Senior Police Officials
dealing with the case were 'frankly
baffled' as to who could do this.
Supa Scoop's reporter comments:

> This is no mere petty break-in.
> Here was a defenceless woman,
> frail, old, well-liked, partly crippled,
> living on her Old Age Pension,
> living all alone, her only
> company an ageing cage-bird,
> scalded, beaten, slashed, hair pulled out,
> fingers broken – her assailants
> making off (when, quite unable
> to supply them information
> as to any 'hoard of savings',
> she fell at their feet unconscious),
> making off with £1.60,
> making off with £1.60,
> *making off with £1.60*
> and a box of CHOCKO YUM-YUMS.

*

In the tray of sand and faeces
at the bottom of the bird-cage
it spins rhythmically on one wing
where a stump of singed flight-feathers
joins a dislocated shoulder.
All the primaries are burnt off.
It emits a hissing whisper
'Hello sailor. Hello sailor.'
Slowly, nictitating membranes
squeeze across dull-bloomed sclerotics.

*

When she opened up the front door
Gibbo punched her in the guts like,
give her head-butts, dragged her screamin
into the front room. I says 'Look,
where's yer bleedin money, Mrs?'
She says nuffink so I rubs these
chocolates what she had hard in her
face like. Then we gets this knife thing
what she had hung on the wall like
and we gives her face the old quick
criss-cross with the point. She gives us
all this crap: 'Wah-wah, you demons,
have you no love for your mothers?'
So I gives her hair a bleedin
pull what sent her screamin. It was
dead great, how she screamed and screamed and
how her hair come out in handfuls.
Gibbo gets this bleedin budgie
what she had in this big cage thing
and he got its wings and lit them
with his old fag-lighter. It was
dead great how that parrot-thing went
up in smoke. Gib bit its beak off.
That was dead great, how he done it.
Then we found her purse and all it
had was bleedin one pound fifty
so we give her fingers the old
snap-snap like and Gibbo tells her

222

'If you don't say where you've got it
hid, I'll give ya boilin water.'
And he did. That was dead great like.
There was dates – I don't like them much.

Mynah Petrarchan *

What a big fellow *he* is for his age!
Give us a drink. I likes a drop of rum.
Hello there, sailor boy! Who loves his mum?
Look at that bird! Let's stuff it full of sage
and onion! Cocky's out on the rampage!
Everyone loves black Cocky! Give us some!
Cocky's a wicked naughty! Smack his bum!
Cocky likes nice boys. Lock him in his cage.

Cocky must stay inside. Sit on his perch.
Speak to me, Cocky. Say a little wordie.
Give us a kiss, then. Who's a pretty boy?
What would poor mummy do left in the lurch?
What if the bad boys got her little birdie?
Where would she be without her pride and joy?

* Declaimed by Oriental passerine.

After Sanraku Koshu

Jailed for being drunk,
but far from contrite, the bard,
minus shoes, tie, belt,
savoured steel grille, rank pallet,
mused 'Ah! Raw Material!'

Sortie

'Didn't you hear about it? Well, as planned, he
went up to Town and lunched quite well at Wheeler's –
Pol Roger '71 with half a dozen
large Irish oysters, fine bottle of Clicquot
'75 with a dressed lobster, '60
Dow's with a Stilton. Looked up Stinker's cousin,
drank '63 Warre's with him at the Savile,
then on to Stinker's for Cockburn's '45.
Caught, by mistake, a train to Crewe, where Peelers
found him in deep repose (fatigued by travel
and tiny phials of Inter-City brandy).
Night spent in durance vile. Next day the beak – "Oh,
tell me, are you drunk frequently?" He fixed the
ass with a scowl and got quite haughty – "I've
never touched Strong Drink (but for a Christmas Fino)."
£10. Quite an amusing little beano.'

15th February

I tried to put in what I really felt.
I really tried to put in what I felt.
I really felt it – what I tried to put.
I put it really feelingly, or tried.
I felt I really tried to put it in.
What I put in I tried to really feel.
Really I felt I'd tried to put it in.
I really tried to feel what I put in.

It cost £5 in WH Smith's.
£5 it cost – WH Smith's ain't cheap.
£5 ain't cheap, not for a thing like that.
It costs, a thing like that – £5 ain't cheap.
It wasn't a cheap thing – £5 it cost.
A thing like that ain't cheap in WH Smith's.
In WH Smith's a thing like that comes costly.
A lot to pay, £5, for a thing like that.

The heart was scarlet satin, sort of stuffed.
I sort of felt it was me own heart, like.
SHE TORE THE STUFFING OUT OF THE SCARLET HEART.
I sort of stuffed and tore her sort of scarlet.
I stuffed her, like, and felt her sort of satin.
I sort of felt she'd tore out all me stuffing.
I felt her stuff like satin sort of scarlet
her stuff felt sore, torn satin whorlet scar
I liked her score felt stiffed her scar lick hurt
I tore her satin felt her stuffed her scarlet
tore out her heart stuff scarred her Satan har
I licked her stiff tore scarf her harlot hair
tied scarf tore stabbed scar whore sin sat tit star
stuffed finger scar ha ha ha ha ha ha
felt stiff scarf tight tore scarlet heart her scare
her scare stare stabbed heart scarlet feel torn mur

Found

Strange find – a plastic dummy from a boutique
(boots, white long thighs, pants pulled right down, a sack
over the head and torso) dumped among bins
and tumps of fetid garbage and coils of rank
sloppy dog faeces in an ill-lit alley
between the Launderette and Indian Grocer.
Incorrect diagnosis: it emits
a high-pitched rattle like Callas gargling.

Rescrutinising 36 hours later:
what was, in sodium light, viridian,
is, in pale February sun, maroon.
About a soup-cupful remains still viscous,
black at the rim where a scabbed mongrel sniffs,
ripples taut sinew, salivates and laps.

Stedman's

I am going to write a sonnet
concerning Huntington's Chorea
from the viewpoint of a Year 2
Pharmacy student, and so
I am looking up **Chorea** in
Stedman's Medical Dictionary.

On the same page as I require,
this appears: **Choreophrasia-**
The continual repetition
of meaningless phrases.

                    I wonder
if I ought, after all, to despatch
the pharmacist's Granny by means of
convulsions, or whether to have her
reduced to a jabbering night-hag
whose terminal speech* could be rendered
with agreeable anarchy.

In *A Sort of Life*, Greene remarked
(mitigating the relish with which
he observed parental distress
at the death of a ten-year-old)
'There is a splinter of ice
in the heart of a writer.'

                              I savour
the respective merits of one
kind of mayhem over another,
contentedly ponder the species
of fourteen-liner most apposite –
Petrarchan? Elizabethan?

---

*   Carew, Carew, Carew, my bonny lad.
Where do we go from here? Brisk cockatoo.
Happy the man who knows not he is glue.
Which way? Which way? I love Jahanabad
in Spring. What drunken bard? An ironclad
means tank. My bonny lad. Carew, Carew.
From here we venture to the Portaloo
of death. Brisk cockatoo is very bad!
        I had a Polly budgie in a box.
Seagull and fox. Paisley is *not* OK.
Carew, Carew, Carew, cock, cocky, cocky.
These sweets are jolly fudgy. Chicken Pox!
These literary magazines are fey,
cock, cocky, cock. Carew. I hates a trochee!

A Recollection

She always was a great one for the pranks.
We hadn't seen her for about 5 years.
To find her in that place with all those cranks
was like one of her jokes – we laughed till our tears
unfocused her as she winked, twitched and flexed
her limbs. Then we saw that she was weeping too,
realised the reason for the high-walled, annexed,
discreetly-labelled building.

                    Sleeping through
most of the morning's 2nd Year Pharmacy,
he emerged drowsily, heard, as in a dream,
'...Huntington's Chorea. Though, when calmer, she
exhibited no more symptoms than extreme
involuntary twitching...' and recalled
the childhood visit and was newly appalled.

Nips

Look at the high tor!
The rocks are older than men
and will last longer.

Thank you very much
for pointing this out to us,
PBS Spring Choice.

                  *

Crossing the campus
with a 6 by 6 canvas
in a force 7,
the art student looks like a
discomfited Wright brother.

His large oil depicts
a seagull in a tweed suit
boxing with a fox
who wears muffler and flat cap.
(An allegory, I think.)

*

Touching to see men
normally at variance
unite (in whining
about meagre salaries
at the Faculty Meeting).

*

The Prime Minister
is an incompetent fool,
Rustics are bumpkins,
Townies are corrupt. I am
a good man and know what's what.

*

In last week's press, X
reviewed Y: *One of the best
poets now writing.*

In this week's press, Y
reviews X: *One of the best
poets writing now.*

*

Not Nell Gwynn (alas),
but the intense, short, hirsute
editor of *Stand*
importunes our theatre queue –
'Come! Buy my juicy lit. mags!'

*

Phoney-rustic bards,
spare us your thoughts about birds,
butterflies, fish, snakes
and mammals (including us) –
biologists write more sense.
Down the lab they think
these crows, peasants, pikes, eels, swifts
are twee, ill-observed.

Bumpkins, from whose bums
you consider the sun shines,
think you're townee twits.
Like that haiku frog,
unscientific fauna
is a bore in verse.

Ex Lab

I

Dilute acetic
has exposed from the matrix
(limestone, Jurassic),
ischium and ilium
and interlocking pubis.

These demonstrate how
ornithischian hip joints
differ from those of
saurischians. These bits are
believed *Scelidosaurus*.

After coffee-break
they will be made ready for
hardening resin.
           These flimsy inked surfaces
           come from the Late Holocene:

           CIRCUS STRONG-WOMAN
           CONVICTED OF MANSLAUGHTER.
           STUDENT 'GOES MISSING'
           IN AFRICAN MYSTERY.
           SKINHEAD SETS FIRE TO CAGE-BIRD.

In what's now Dorset
one hundred and eighty-five
million years ago,
Megalosaurus et al
flenched, flensed these bastards to mince.

II

I am cleaning up
a piece of dinosaur shit
(Upper Cretacious,
length 20 centimetres)
that came from Mongolia.

Someone else requires
the air-abrasive machine
urgently. I stop
and peruse my copy of
a Nietzsche biography.

> Up to a point, yes.
> 'God is dead' – quite straightforward.
> But why, then, go on
> to think some mitigation
> is needed for us to face
>
> Godless cosmic dust?
> Matter just gets on with it.
> Saying 'YES to life',
> conceiving 'Übermenschen'
> is an arrogant sell-out
>
> quite as fey as 'God'.
> Anyway, Nietzsche was nuts –
> got stopped by the fuzz
> for taking off his clothing
> and bathing in a puddle.

This one matrix holds
fragments of eggshell (believed
Protoceratops –
about ninety million years
of age) and a turd fossil.

I believe in this:
no übermenschen's remnant
(not one coprolite)
is going to be better
than this elegant stone crap.

III

Is Sin Sinful*ness?*
preoccupies my pious
colleagues over lunch.
Hydrogen and Helium –
the Original Sinners.

On this diagram
(chrono-stratigraphical),
3.6 billion
years ago may be seen as
about the start of Earth life.

When your daughter dies
aged ten, mown down by a train,
console yourself thus:
sky-pilots can forgive her
by saying a Special Thing.

On this diagram,
the Holocene or Recent
(last ten thousand years)
is far, far, far, far too small
to register on this scale.

You live, then you die.
This is extremely simple.
You live, then you die –
no need to wear funny hats,
no need for mumbo-jumbo.

IV

The '62 find,
Heterodontosaurus
(southern Africa,
Upper Trias), concerned me
greatly because of the *teeth*

(rather than because
Scelidosaurus had been
the earliest known
ornithischian till then) –
that almost 'canine' 'eye-tooth'!

　　　　Oozing bonhomie,
　　　　we take unwanted knick–knacks
　　　　to the Oxfam shop –
　　　　at last! the starving millions
　　　　will have a nice bite to eat!

The stomach contents
of an *Anatosaurus*
I am working on
were mummified – pine-needles
seventy million years old.

　　　　In Belfast, I read,
　　　　the craze is for hunger-strikes.
　　　　Eat your porridge up
　　　　like good little murderers
　　　　(Political Status, balls).

These five gastroliths
(stomach-stones to grind food) were
worn smooth as pool balls
by an unknown sauropod
of the Upper Jurassic.

Called to specialise
in one stratigraphical
field, I decided
the Late Holocene (*our* scene)
did not concern me greatly.

V

At the end of the
Cretacious, a 'Great Dying'
seems to have occurred,
when half of all animal
and plant groups became extinct.

That extinction seems
to have been protracted for
a few million years;
this one, now underway, will
have reached a similar scale

in a few decades.
The hiatus resulting
in some processes
of evolution will be
extremely fascinating.

> 'SUPER-TANKA SINKS'
> (the misprint suggests Baroque,
> fugal, cumbersome
> development of the Five-
> Seven-Five-Seven-Seven...).

What one enjoys most
is the manipulation
of these hapless things
at such impartial distance
to fit an imposed order.

Of course one does not
really care for the *objects*,
just the *subject*. It
is a Vulture Industry,
cashing in on the corpses.

Vacuum, cosmic dust,
algae, rhipidistians,
internecine us
(it is a fucking good job
that it all does not matter).

From a Journal

(c. 1917, in the author's possession)

My Grandfather knew Gideon Algernon Mantell
(discoverer of the Iguanodon*)*
who shewed him, in 1822, in Sussex,
those teeth! of creatures hitherto undreamed-of.

My Grandfather, in 1841,
was at the B.A.A.S. Plymouth meeting*
when Doctor (later Prof, Sir) Richard Owen
unleashed the Dinosaur on smug Victorians.

My Grandfather, a polymath, drew well,
botanised, 'Englished' Vergil, geologised.
My Grandfather was born in 1800,
Father in 1850, I myself
in 1895...

He would have been
88 (but for 1917).

Englished (ii. 458)

Far from the clash of Celt twerps,
        the Barley Mow telly transmits
atrocities none of the rustics
        attends to lest they eclipse
his own catalogue of woes –
        the price of bag-muck increases,
Hill Subsidies insufficient
        to run the Merc and the Rover.

---

* At the 1841 Plymouth meeting of the British Association for the Advancement of Science, Owen (1804-1892), first Director of the Natural History Museum in South Kensington, suggested that *Iguanodon*, *Megalosaurus* and *Hylacosaurus* should together be named the Dinosauria, the 'terrible lizards'.

The muggings, the dole queues, the miners
(audaciously asking for more)
are ignored; the new Combine is costing
(Nat-West) 46 grand,
masonry bees are molesting
the Georgian brick of the Glebe.
Salopian swains make merry
with rough rhymes and boisterous mirth.

O fortunatos nimium,
suà si bona norint...
– farmers are fortunate fuckers,
wanting the wit to know it.

[Shropshire, July 1981]

Englished (iii. 349-83)

Winter is simply beastly for northern neatherds,
girt in the smelly pelts of Reynard and Ursa,
crouched in uncomfy igloos killing time swilling
gassy cyder and frothy Bass and frolicking.

Boreas's eastern child whines incessantly.
You could drive your muck-spreader on the icèd tarn.
The kine are all dead and under 7 cubits
of snow. The antlery tribes are stuck numb in drifts.

Your duds freeze stiff as you stand by the elm log blaze.
Brazen knick-knacks from Brum burst asunder with cold.
Icicles crackle in uncombed hairies' beavers.
It's really really rotten to be Rhyphaean.

Oenophiles give you Grands Crus by weight, not volume,
cleaving the frozen Lafite with their tomahawks.

[Tyne & Wear, January 1982]

237

Epithalamium

I

…have great pleasure in…
of their daughter Crystal…
enclosed Gift List…

> Dragonstraw door mat in plaited seagrass
> from China.
> 'Tik Tok' wall clock, battery-operated
> quartz movement in pine frame.
> 'La Primula Stripe' dishwasher-proof
> glazed earthenware coffee set.
> Valance with neat box pleats to fit
> 3ft to 5ft beds (fixed by Velcro pads).
> Michel Guérard's kitchen work table
> with base of solid pine, including
> a duckboard shelf for storage,
> a knife rack and pegs for teacloths.
> Boxwood pastry crimper.
> 'Confucius' 50% polyester,
> 50% cotton duvet cover.
> Pine wine rack.
> Pine lavatory paper holder.
> Solid pine toilet seat with chrome fittings
> (coated with 6 layers of polyurethane).
> Iron omelette pan with curved sides.
> Angus Broiler cast iron pan for steaks
> and chops which combines the ease of frying
> with the goodness of grilling.
> 'Leonardo' sofa in cream herringbone.
> Honey-coloured beech bentwood rocker
> with cane back and seat.
> Cork ice-bucket with aluminium insert.
> 'Mr Toad' rattan chair from France.
> Tough cotton canvas Sagbag filled
> with flame-retardant polystyrene granules.

II

The fizz is Spanish, labelled 'MEGOD CHAMPAIN'.

III

...have great pleasure in...
will now read Greetings Cards...

> de da de da de da de da this wedding gift to you
> de da de da de da de da your golden years come true...
> All the way from America...
> sorry can't be there...
> would love to have been there...
> a California 'Howdy!'...
> de da de da de da de da all your hopes and fears
> de da de da de da de da throughout the coming years...

HA HA HA HA HA HA HA (what a riot the Best Man *is*).

IV

At their new home – 'Crimmond' (next to 'Sinatra' on one side
and 'Mon Rêve' on the other) – the presents are laid out.
They look lovely, don't they, Confucius, Leonardo and Mr
Toad.

V

Bog paper and boots are tied to their bumper.
Consummation in Calais is nothing to write home about.

Carte Postale

Dear Mum and Dad,
                    The picture shows a 'gendarme'
which means policeman. France is overrated.
For two weeks it has been wet. 9th September:
we had a 'dégustation' in the Côte
de Mâconnais and Mal got quite light-headed.
Sometimes I think it will be *too* ideal
living with Mal – it's certainly the Real
Thing. I must go now – here comes Mal.
                                    Love, Crystal.

Encircling her slim waist with a fond arm,
the husband of a fortnight nibbles her throat,
would be dismayed to learn how she had hated
that first night when in Calais he had kissed all
over her, and, oh God!, how she now dreaded
each night the importunate mauve-capped swollen member.

Between the Headlines

(Not if she knew her X-ray result.)
STAR QUITS HOSPITAL CURED

(Not acrimonious veg
but internecine Celts.)
GREENS CLASH WITH ORANGES

*(Not like a mongrel picking up spare bones,
I try to photograph wars with compassion*
opines McCullin* on purveying mayhem.)
BABY SHOT IN BELLY

* Declared by *Newsweek* 'the greatest battlefield photographer of our time'.

240

(Not democratic: on Election Day,
soldiers, the oldest of them about 15,
dispose of corpses at the polling booths
then resume licking their lollipops.)
30,000 CIVILIANS CLAIMED

(Not nice Nips send huge
vessel containing crude-oil
to drive imported
Yamahas and Suzukis
and bugger up your beaches.)
SUPER TANKA SINKS – SLICK SLAYS SEAGULLS

(Not had such a supper in their life
and the little ones chewed on the bones-o
bones-o
bones-o
not had such a supper in their life
and the little ones chewed on the bones-o.)
STUDENT 'GOES MISSING' IN AFRICAN MYSTERY

(Not-Foreskin v Foreskin –
Old Testament berks
in daft dressing-gowns
and peep-toe slippers
play atavistic
grenade-lobbing pranks
in the Holy Land.)
SALAAM/SHALOM SHAM

(Not to be regarded
as more than a physiological
characteristic – a big brain
does not mean specific aloofness.
Don't think *thinking* makes you
different from, say, rhipidistians.
Souls/arse-holes are the same stuff –
very thin stripes in a tall cliff.)
PORTALOO CLAIMS FOSSIL PROF

Admissions

Both were unconscious on arrival, one
with serious head injuries, the other
with broken back and ribs and damaged pelvis
(they were put with the factory accident
who'd been admitted earlier with a severed
arm, only 16, he died later too).
Both had been injured when a lorry shed
its load of Portaloo site-lavatories
impartially on a bus queue. One of them,
a circus tightrope-walker, sat bolt upright,
bowed, burst into floods of tears and then expired
wheezing 'Miss Jill! Miss Jill! Miss Jill!'. The other,
a palaeontologist, died screaming out
'THE HOLOCENE DID NOT CONCERN ME GREATLY!'

Finds

I

The *Mammuthus*, winched from the permafrost
during the famous Schmitstein expedition
of '51, was truly magnificent,
the finest-preserved specimen yet found –
tusks 4.8 m, 3.3 at shoulder.

It was transported, carefully supervised
by scientists from the Ghustphsen Institute,
back to the base at Skruskhev where impromptu
laboratory facilities were installed.

One of the expedition's porters owned
a husky of unprepossessing aspect.
One night it gained admission to the lab
and ate the 20,000-year-old trunk.

II

The Schneider had one 75 mm
gun, also two machine guns. Double armour
plates on the front, the sides and top. These plates
were separated with a 1.5
inch space between them. Armour varied from
.2 inches to .95 inches.
Maximum speed about 5 miles per hour.
Vertical coil springs, jointed bogie frames.
Tracks – solid plates with single grousers, width
was 14 inches, pitch 10 inches. Length
19 feet 8, width 6 feet 7, height
7 feet 10. Weight 14.9 tons.
A Schneider 70 horse-power water-cooled
4 cylinder engine. There were sliding gears,
3 forward, 1 reverse. Range – 25
miles on a fuel tank holding 53
gallons. Equipped with double tailpiece. Nose
intended as wire-cutter and to assist
in crossing obstacles. Unditching beam
carried on right side. Dome ventilating louvre
on top of hull. The overhanging hull
greatly reduced rough-ground mobility.
Vertical armour plates could not withstand
thc celebrated German bullet the 'K'.

A nasty versifier is researching,
sniffing historic carnage, adding salt...

Resolution

When the French tank the *Schneider* was introduced
(capable of 6 kilometres per hour,
weight 15 tons, guns 75 mm)
in the bright April sun of '17,
a subaltern watched two tree-pipits ascend
from the black jagged shelled limbs of a pine
and entered sundry commonplaces in this
journal – concluding with the desultory

Watched pipits' song-flight. Saw new ironclad
capable of 6 kilometres per hour,
weight 15 tons, guns 75 mm.
Tonight, after lights-out, I am resolved,
although I love you, Sally, to lie brow-down
on a grenade and then to detonate it.

Tryst

Me and Gib likes it here – always comes of a night,
no one else gets here, see. That's his Great-Grandad's stone.
Gassed, *he* was; got sent home from one of them *old* wars.
                    Tommy, they called him.

We sprayed HARTLEPOOL WANKERS on one of them. Great!
This is the newest one – sad it is, really, it's
some little ten-year-old girlie's. Them plastic daffs
                    look very nice, though.

He likes to get me down in the long weeds between
two of them marble things – I can see ivy sprout
on the cross by his head. He makes me squiggle when
                    he sticks his hand up.

He works at one of them mills what makes cattle food.
He stacks the sacks. You should see them tattoos on his
arms when he flexes them. There is a big red heart
                    with TRUE LOVE on it.

He runs the Packer-thing all on his own, he does.
We're saving up to get married and have a big
do like that big snob that works in our office had
                    (Crystal, her name is).

I let him do what he wants – he pretends that he's
the Ripper, sometimes, and gets me down on a grave;
then what he does with his hands feels like scurrying
                    rats up my T-shirt.

When we've saved up enough, we're going to wed in church.
This is all right, though – at least in the summertime.
They don't pay poor Gib much, stacking them heavy sacks
                    off the conveyor.

Pacepacker

THE *PACEPACKER* NEEDS ONE OPERATOR ONLY.
PLACE EMPTY PAPER SACKS IN RACK MARKED 'SACKS',
ENSURING THEY ARE CLAMPED TIGHT WITH SPRING CLAMP.
ADJUST CONVEYERS TO CORRECT HEIGHTS. SWITCH ON.
WHEN 'START RUN' LIGHT SHOWS GREEN, PRESS 'START RUN' BUTTON.
SACKS ARE PICKED UP BY SUCKERS, STITCHED AND CONVEYED
TO ELEVATOR. ENSURE CLOTHING AND HANDS
ARE CLEAR OF CONVEYOR BELT.

                          The corrugated
rapidly-moving strip of rubber seemed
to draw the arm smoothly, unresistingly
up through the oiled steel rollers. The 'Stop Run' light
shows red. The matt belt glistens where a smear
of pink mulch, fatty lumps, flensed skin, singed hair,
is guzzled dry by plump impartial houseflies.

5 x 5 x 5 x 5 x 5

(1983)

5x5x5x5x5 was conceived as a collaboration with artist David Butler, and originally published with his images. It consists of 5 sections, each section of 5 units, each unit 5 stanzas, each stanza 5 lines, each line 5 syllables (there is one hypercatalectic line in 2 v). 5 personae are observed in 5 (licensed) locations.

A dead wombat, stuffed
with contemptuous
disregard for all
anatomical
possibility,

is nailed to a beam
with a Davy lamp
and a World War 1
gas-mask and a glass
fashioned like a boot.

Utterly morose
after eight of Bass,
I review the gross
sub-species and freaks
swilling at the bar.

Those most loth to wash
breed most rapidly –
ghastly extras from
some Fellini film.
Working, as I do,

with Precambrian
specimens aged six
hundred million years
sires irreverence
for the Holocene.

1 II

This is a very
democratic Lounge:
Schultz lectures Logic,
Fats is a binman.
Fats gulps Mild. Schultz pays.

Schultz sips dry Vermouth.
They are both crackers.
'Conceive, if you will,
that the number 2
is blue, 3 yellow...'

Fats sniffs his empty,
adjusts his tweed cap,
is given more Mild.
'Conceive, if you will – '
but Fats's brain reels...

    4 and 5 Minstrels,
    Blue Lovely 4 Eyes,
    Tie a 3 Ribbon,
    1 Grow the Rushes,
    Bluety-Green Today,

    That Coal-4 Mammy,
    Green Man Went to Mow,
    Baby's Got 2 Eyes,
    1, 1 Grass of Home
    and *Yellow Blind Mice...*

Agotta faggal
fagoffa lager
egg offal agarr
gag ottle og ear
a gottle of gear

>Once upon a time
>e were right famous
>ventriloquister,
>played all the Big Spots
>(the *Rex*, the *Empire*),
>
>called isself The Great
>Maestro De La Voice
>(once e played before
>the Lady Mayoress
>of Middlesbrough).
>
>What e used to do
>were make this doll speak
>wi a dead queer voice –
>bloody great, it were –
>just like *it* talkin.
>
>Now e gets a bit,
>you know, tiddly,
>gets mixed up between
>what e *used* to say
>on the Stage and *now*.

'Jishcumm backfrumm thee
Musee yum, my dear,'
the technician from
the museum lab
confides to his spouse.

It is midnight and,
for his birthday treat,
she has had a *Boeuf*
au je ne sais quoi
bubbling since 6.

She is not much pleased.
First she bellows (loud)
'■■* ʒ ℞ *!*
HAVE YOU BEEN TILL NOW?!'
Then she gently weeps.

Something has gone wrong.
'Once there was a time,
when we were first wed,
when you *never* would...
oh, God!, never mind.'

She sprints up to bed.
Something has gone wrong.
He is in the soup.
'Whashummatter, love?
Shummthin darrersed?'

1 v

Jock does Combined Arts.
He's a Second Year
and plays in defence
for the Poly team.
God!, he makes you laugh.

He's just sunk six pints
of Low C Draught Pils
and he needs a wee –
calls it 'Shaking hands
with the Unemployed'.

After being sick
in the bog, he writes,
in green felt-tip on
a machine that sells
contraceptives, quips:

THIS MACHINE DEGRADES
WOMEN SO DO I
THESE BALLOONS DON'T WORK
GUARANTEED 9 MONTHS
BUY ME AND STOP ONE

(Ho ho what a jape.)
Thus we do our things,
rugger, liquor, ink,
it's a proper lark,
until Closing Time.

...in music-hall days
we could trick em with
'Gredd and gutter' – see?–
distance it was. Nah,
telly spoiled all that...

...conceive, if you will,
does red have a *size?*
Can I win a prize
on this fruit-machine
when it is not here?...

...downed a few last night,
late back, supper burnt,
she said 'You think more
of those ammonites
than of me'. (Dead right.)...

...ang on, wait a jiff:
if it isn't ere
ow the bleedin ell
canyer winna prize?
Wish I ad a pint...

...so we're in the showers
an ah held it up
shoutin 'Who's is this?
Who's got thirty-eights?'
Bluidy laugh, ye ken...

2 II

...'member Fred Russell?
Father of Modern
Ventriloquism –
is dummy was called
Coster Joe. One time[2]

...I do not doubt, Fats,
that you are *au fait*
with recent work by
Rescher and Brandom[1]
on *Realism*...

...thirty-eight, I am,
birthday yesterday,
married fifteen years –
the Oligocene
engages me more...

...you know, Mr Shoots,
you're a genius,
jay-ee-en-eye-uss
genius, you are.
Don't mind if I do...

...phoned me up, ye ken,
said 'I wuddna ask
anyone but you.
I'm *dying* for it.'
She's a smart chick, mind...

2 III

...they thought Fred Russell
was the first to use
a knee-figure – *but*
Fred Neiman was first
– 1892...[2]

...if it's 6 o'clock
you can hear the News;
if you hear the News
you have ears. Therefore
if it's 6 you've ears...[3]

...I was reading in
Special Papers how
two localities
have produced five types
of fossil cichlid...[4]

...I admire you
Mr Shoo, you know,
as for Rasher an
Randy, well, you see,
mine's a pish of Mile...

...I'm a great one for
the lasses, ye ken,
I'll show ye how te
chat em up 'A reet
daerlin, gerremdoun...'

2 IV

...there's a photo shows
Fred Neiman using
that knee-figure in
'Prof' Anderson's show
'Wizard of the North'...[2]

...if he dies tonight
he will visit us
tomorrow; because
he will visit us
tomorrow – you see?...[3]

...the herbivorous
cichlids first appear
at Rusinga in
Early Miocene[4] –
have another Bass?...

...wash *I* wisha know,
how to win the prishe
when there no mashee
when no froo machine.
Wish I pint os Milsd...

...'A reet, lassie, noo,
getcher knickersdoun'
ha ha ha ha ha
ha ha ha ha ha,
bluidy laugh, ye ken?...

...'member Johnson Clark?
used to dress up like
a posh country gent,
called his dummy Hodge.
'member 'Prof' D'Alvo?...[2]

...I do not doubt, Fats,
that you are *au fait*
with *Logic and Art* [3]
and the essay by
C.L. Stevenson...

...no pre-Eocene,
nor, preshumabobly,
pre-Oligoshene
speshimens exisht [4] –
mine's another Bash...

...you know, Misha Shooo
I ad mire you,
you are geenius
you are geen geeny
mine is pintamile...

...wusha hadda lass
wush te Goddahad
God ah wush ah had
a wee bonny lass.
God, ah *need* a lass...

3 1

Always amusing,
after a day of
defunct echinites,
to chart the advance
of the sub-species.

Dressed in the kit of
a Full Admiral,
a twerp tells jokes in
Scotch about mammae.
The ventriloquist

and Fats talk Racing.
But the ascendant
are these tattooed Skins,
LOVE on one fist and
HATE on the other,

BAD SKINS RULE in the
strobe's flash and fading.
Quite incongruous,
the highbrow Prof with
Sense of Survival

bred right out of him,
naively chats to
the juke-box on the
theme of *non-standard
possible worlds*. (Gawd.)

& we see   double
& we hear   buzzing
& we feel   dizzy
& we smell   nettles
& we taste   bitter

& we walk   zigzag
& we talk   claptrap
& we think   fuzzy
& we drink   plenty
& we pay   later

& we play   cherries
& we shoot   rapid
& we rock   heavy
& we hit   jackpot
& we jerk   pinball

& we dream   sexy
but we screw   droopy
& we deal   aces
& we dial   happy
but we heal   slowly

& we drool   drippy
& we deal   damsons
& we dial   digits
the machine   rattles
& we die   dippy

3 III

the apparatus
of non-standard poss-
ible worlds as we
have developed it
so far is inval-

uable in the
perspicuous pre-
sentation of an
account of senses,
senses, that is, of

ideality
and reality
whose claim ought to be
adjudicated
in order to set-

tle the issue of
ontological
status. And therefore,
we will use that ap-
aratus to in

some way define the
very notion of
an *inquiry* which
seeks an accurate
and complete repre- [1]

sentation of things
as they really are,
and to define some
constraints on the meth-
odologies which

govern such inquir-
ies as they affect
the reality
which is presumed to
be their subject-mat-

ter. Let us appeal
to the example
of the notable
metaphysical
views of Pierce as a

sound historical
reference-point for a
canvassing of some
neat alternative
metaphysical

views couched in the lang-
uage of non-standard
possible worlds [1] – Ah!
Young men, my friends! Why?
Please, no, please, no, *please!*

get him   in the bogs
shove his   head in it
rub his   face in shit
piss all   over him
get them   matches out

butt him   in the face
knee him   in the crotch
kick him   in the head
smash his   fuckin legs
stick one   in his nuts

posh puff   clever shite
la-de-   fuckin-da
bastard   brainy git
bleedin   college prat
we hate   puffy snobs

boot his   friggin guts
slash him   in the face
slice him   down the neck
get blood   in his eyes
knife his   nose across

set his   coat alight
squash his   other eye
looks like   cherry jam
that should   learn the twat
Bad Skins   Rule OK

Now let's get back to
voice exercises:
we have been learning
to breathe in deeply
and exhale slowly.

Now, while we breathe out,
we will add music.
Sing 'ah' normally.
And now sing 'ah' an
octave higher, but

this time bring the tip
of your tongue down to
below bottom teeth.
This arches your tongue,
pushes the sound back

in your throat and sends
more air through your nose.
This is your first real
ventriloqual sound,
and this is the voice

you'll use when you make
your dummy 'talk'. It
won't *sound* nasal though –
ah ah ah ah ah
ah ah ah ah ah.[2]

While I was cleaning
a Silurian
matrix this morning,
someone informed me
of Schultz's mishap.

The *Railway Hotel*
is thrilled with outrage
as I sip the cure
at lunchtime. The lounge
is called 'FLYING SCOT'.

I see the man 'Fats'
and hail him 'Ah, "Fats",
I learn with dismay
that the simians
ignited your chum.'

His response is 'Eh?'
I repeat 'I say
it's rather hard luck
about Schultz's brush
with the sub-species.'

I notice his specs
are steaming with brine.
He wields a grubby
snot-spattered hanky,
whines 'I *loved* that man'.

4 III

The Formative Minds
are at it again –
exchanging sterile
platitudes, students
sip Pils, wear daft clothes.

One of them yaffles
in gormless Scotch tones
treating of ball games
and cheeky rude pranks –
he's a *fun* person.

Too much confidence,
no respectful fright
or awareness, yet,
of mortality,
too much decibel...

> [Here the author snatched
> up his Bic and scrawled
> on his beer mat:
> *In next Saturday's
> match, regrettably,*
>
> *Jock was savagely
> tackled, losing 8
> teeth, and choking on
> his gum-shield. He died
> in the ambulance.*]

4 IV

We have now to learn
how to say the rest
of the vowels – and watch
lips in the mirror
cos they *must* not move.

You can say 'ah' with
your lips just slightly
parted, but in the
mirror they'll seem closed.
Now try 'ah-ee-ah'.

Don't try to rush things.
It may take many
days or even weeks
to master this. The
most difficult sound

is 'oo' cos your lips
will want to pucker
and form a little
round hole just like this...
When you've mastered it

you can progress to
'ah-ee-oh-ay-oo'
'ah-ee-oh-ay-oo'
'ah-ee-oh-ay-oo'
'ah-ee-oh-ay-oo'.[2]

4 v

In the slopped Guinness
on the counter-top
he traces with his
finger diagrams
for my benefit.

His hows you how hoo
flase your hongue when you
hay he honsonants
EN, ENN, HE, FEE hans,
hars gut hot heast, GEE.

I think Signor Voice,
that I never shall
be requested to
show adroitness in
such specialist skills.

O, I on't ho though!
you hever ho hen
you nay have to hiv
an enherhain-nent
– a girthday, ferhafs?

Would you like more drink?
A gottle of Gass.
In ny old Stage days
hey laughed hill hey hried...
Moved to tears? Yes, yes...

(Carried home last night,
Mrs not too pleased)
pint of Bass please Vi,
that bloke on the wall,
the Thespian snap,

he's got teeth just like
Anachronistes,
genus of shark, I
was dealing with some
this morning, thanks Vi,

let's see how he's signed,
'To Vi with love from
"Dracula" Davis',
yes, well these limestone
specimens come from

Steeplehouse Quarry,
Derbyshire, same place
as Duffin's and Ward's,[5]
Carboniferous
(I say, look at Fats,

apoplectic, eh?,
wouldn't give him more
than a month to go),
they dissolve out with
5% formic...

Cabbage. A cabbage.
They can't do no more.
Ave to spend all is
life in a wheelchair
jabberin nonsense.

Now, then, Mr F,
don't take it so bad.
Is wife brought im round
Tuesday – could be worse.
Drooled is beer, poor soul.

If I got me ands
on them hoogerlums…
After all them things
what e used to speak –
real clever brain power.

What upset me most,
that swine over there –
im as works in the
Nature Museum –
e said *awful* things:

e said 'If e is
jabberin nonsense,
there's no difference
from the way e was
when e was normal.'

...5% formic
should be 'buffered' and
we use calcium
orthophosphate (that
kid from the Poly

looks unwell, and I
feel unwell, weak hearts
in both our cases,
still, what's 40 years
here or there on the

chronostratigraph?),
pint please Vi, it's from
Anachronismos,
out of time, i.e.
early position

of these things in the
stratigraphic chart
(liquor buggers us,
nathless 'Human kind
cannot bear very

much reality'),
there's no accepted
phylogenetic
relevance of shark
tooth morphology.

5 IV

[In a quite unique
collaboration,
Author and Surgeon
today succeeded
in reviving a

hopeless cadaver
killed last Saturday
in the *Wasps'* home match.
Tipp-Ex and scalpel
joined forces to clear

a throat obstruction.
AUTHOR ADMITTED
'I ACTED IN HASTE'.
EX-SCOTTISH PATIENT
EXHUMED AS *ENGLISH*.

NATION-CHANGE DEATH-MAN.
AMBULANCEMEN PRAISED
BY REPENTANT BARD.
DOC'S DEFT KNIFE DELETES
BARD'S HASTY BIC-WORK.]

   'How are you now, Jock?'
   'Perfectly spiffing,
   actually, old thing.
   Awfully eager
   to join the Ladies...'

5 v

Photos line the walls
of the *Theatre Vaults*
signed with things like 'All
luck to Vi and staff
of the Theatre Vaults

from "Cheeky" Chump Chipps'.
One is of a spent
Panto Horse and signed
'From Rick and Gordon –
always a pair for

"horseplay" '. Another
is of a man called
Simon Dee (who was,
some time ago, a
personality).

'Maestro De La Voice,
to all the bar staff;
keep your chin up!' is
curled and nicotined –
he drinks here nightly.

He is here tonight,
sixty-one years old,
at this moment crouched
in the piss-stenched bogs
weeping, and weeping.

REFERENCES

1. *The Logic of Inconsistency* (Rescher & Brandom, Blackwell, 1980), section 20, 'Methodological Realism and the Convergence of Inquiry'.

2. *Ventriloquism for Beginners: A Complete Set of Lessons in the Art of Voice Magic* (Douglas Houlden, AIMC, Kaye & Ward, 1958).

3. *Logic & Art* (ed. Rudner & Scheffler, Bobbs-Merrill Co. Inc., 1972), essay by Charles L. Stevenson 'If-iculties'.

4. *Special Papers in Palaeontology*, No. 29 'Fossil Cichlid Fish of Africa' (Judith Anne Harris Van Couvering, The Palaeontological Association, London, 1982), p. 96, 'Phylogenetic & Evolutionary Implications'.

5. *Palaeontology*, Vol. 26 Part 1, 'Neoselachian Sharks' Teeth from the Lower Carboniferous of Britain...' (Duffin & Ward, The Palaeontological Association, 1983).

NOTES

1. '...as a "Voice Magician" but had not worked for many years. Letters were found to his friends and even one to the coroner – "To make your task easier". He fixed electrodes to his body but left a warning notice "Danger! Do not touch my body until you have switched off the current". The coroner remarked "Despite the macabre nature of his death, he died with dignity. Even at the end he took precautions lest anyone be hurt dismantling the electrodes. He was a man who always lived by the maxim 'the show must go on'.".' (*Evening Advertiser*, 5 February 1983)

2. W.P.C. Elliott is quoted in the *Cheltenham Chronicle* of 17th January 1983 as stating: 'The accused appeared from behind His 'n' Hers Boutique and began spitting on, kicking and abusing a man in a wheelchair who repeatedly screamed out "Possible worlds, possible worlds, possible worlds, possible worlds" as if he was incapable of coherent speech.'

3. 'Both had been injured when a lorry shed its load of Portaloo site lavatories impartially on a bus queue. ...The other, a palaeontologist, died screaming out THE HOLOCENE DID NOT CONCERN ME GREATLY!' (*Diplopic*, P. Reading, Secker & Warburg, 1983).

4. 'Ferdie "Fats" Oliver is the first to take advantage of the Council Employees' SLIM FOR HEALTH campaign. 19 stone Ferdie says "I started to slim because my doctor said I was overweight and my heart was suffering." 20-pint-a-night Ferdie has already lost 16 pounds!' (*Evening Advertiser*, 5 February 1983).

5. A headline in the *Evening Advertiser* of February 5th 1983 reads POLY STUDENT DIES IN DEATH-MATCH TACKLE (this, apparently, in blatant contravention of the author's earlier magnanimous decision to revoke sentence).

C

(1984)

*(Incongruously I plan
100 100-word units.)*

The brass plate polished wordless. Stone steps hollowed by the frightened hopeful ascending, the terrified despairing descending. (Probably between three and four months, perhaps one hundred days.) Out of the surgeries in this Georgian street, and similar streets in similar cities, some of us issue daily, bearing the ghastly prognostications. How we hate you, busy, ordinary, undying – taxi-driver, purveyor of the *Evening Star*, secretary bouncing puddings of malleable flesh. Incongruously I plan 100 100-word units. What do you expect me to do – break into bloody haiku?

> Verse is for healthy
> arty-farties. The dying
> and surgeons use prose.

* * *

The Whale is situated on the quay and is used by ferrymen and travellers calling for a quick drink before crossing. The Colliers is frequented by men from the pit. The fellow known as Tucker regularly attends both establishments. Perhaps he is in charge of the turnstile, the palm of his hand constantly grey from receiving pennies. Or he may be a gypsy, for he deals, apparently, in horses. He addressed me one evening in the bar of the Whale with importunate familiarity, remarking that I might henceforward know him as 'Char' (short for 'Charlie'?) or 'Mort' (short for 'Mortimer'?).

* * *

McGill-Melzack Pain Questionnaire word descriptors for scoring methods:

Flickering, Quivering, Pulsing, Throbbing, Beating, Pounding, Jumping, Flashing, Shooting, Pricking, Boring, Drilling, Stabbing. Lancinating, Sharp, Cutting, Lacerating, Pinching, Pressing, Gnawing, Cramping, Crushing, Tugging, Pulling, Wrenching, Hot, Burning, Scalding, Searing, Tingling, Itchy, Smarting, Stinging, Dull, Sore, Hurting, Aching, Heavy, Tender, Taut, Rasping, Splitting, Tiring, Exhausting, Sickening, Suffocating, Fearful, Frightful, Terrifying, Punishing, Gruelling, Cruel, Vicious, Killing, Wretched, Blinding, Annoying, Troublesome, Miserable, Intense, Unbearable, Spreading, Radiating, Penetrating, Piercing, Tight, Numb, Drawing, Squeezing, Tearing, Cool, Cold, Freezing, Nagging, Nauseating, Agonising, Dreadful, Torturing.

Present Pain Intensity (PPI) intensity scale:

No Pain, Mild, Discomforting, Distressing, Horrible, Excruciating.

* * *

Disseminated spinal carcinoma.
I have lost all control and movement of
the abdomen, legs, feet and back. The growth
(particularly painful) on the spine
prevents my lying on my back. Bedsores
daily increase in size, restrict still more
manipulation of me on the bed –
nurses change my position every hour.
The open bedsores suppurate and stink...
I am abusive to a social worker.

We, trained Caregivers, can identify
symptoms like this – he is withdrawn and craves
attentive sympathy. Each afternoon
I persist – my ability to bear
his poor responses helps him to contain
his desperation. So there is much comfort.

* * *

When I was a boy and read that section at the end of Book V where shipwrecked Laertides crawls under two close-growing olives, one wild one cultivated, exhausted and finds shelter, I was deeply and permanently influenced. Since then the idea of such a comforting and comfortable solitary and impregnable bower has been inseparable for me from the concept of profound sweet sleep – and more... Almost every night since that time, except when drunken or erotic diversion has rendered such conceit impracticable, I have snuggled into the warm bedlinen metamorphosing it to dry Sabaean insulating leaves, blanding approaching oblivion.

* * *

[He breaks down and sobs embarrassingly.] The helpless things people scream out so childishly helplessly like 'Oh please I don't want to die I don't want to die I don't *want* to die!' Well, I scream them now I DON'T *WANT* TO   OH HELP ME PLEASE I DON'T *WANT* TO DIE I. [Drivel.] Why write it? Why ever wrote any of it? Poetry all weak lies, games. Epicurus, stupid lies, that there is nothing terrible in not living. Just to stay oh living, oh, why can't I? Stupid childish helpless poor little frightened [Pusillanimous drivel.] frail poor me. Us *all*.

* * *

Verse unvindicable; therefore sublate *The Ballad of Tucker's Tale* (It's once he was a welterweight/And mingled with the champs/ But now he isn't fit, they say,/To make arse-holes for tramps – / Kips in the Council's GRIT FOR ROADS/Fibreglass yellow bin/And Tucker's Tale's known from the Whale/To the Canny Colliers Inn ...). During the war, Tucker's squad, randy in France, was queuing up to shag a goat. A lance-corp jumped the queue. Everyone complained, but, while the offender was on the job, his head split suddenly apart leaking grey and crimson. Sniper. Vita brevis; ars ditto.

* * *

Twenty of them. Should be sufficient. Comforting rattle from the brown plastic bottle. Twist of cotton wool. Label typed ONLY AS DIRECTED. Wrapped in linen in the rucksack: the decanter engraved with my initials, the eighteenth-century twist-stemmed glass, the last bottle of 1894 Bual. Yapsel Bank, Hanging Brink, Ashes Hollow, Grindle Nills, Long Synalds. A good enough place to go stiff in. Quite unattended now, on hills where once my sweet wife, my dear daughter...(enough of that shite). Oakleymill Waterfall. Skewered by evening sun. Fat, buttery fumosity of amber decanted Madeira. Sour chalkiness of the twentieth pillule.

* * *

I used to pepper my poetics with sophisticated allusions to *dear* Opera and *divine* Art (one was constantly reminded of A. du C. Dubreuil's libretto for Piccinni's *Iphigenia in Tauris*; one was constantly reminded of Niccolò di Bartolomeo da Foggia's bust of a crowned woman, doubtless an allegory of the Church, from the pulpit of Ravello cathedral, *ca.* 1272) but suddenly these are hopelessly inadequate. Where is the European cultural significance of tubes stuck up the nose, into the veins, up the arse? A tube is stuck up my prick, and a bladder carcinoma diagnosed. One does not recall Piccinni.

* * *

My husband never once entertained the notion of transcendentalism. He regarded it as an arrogant ('arrogant humility' is a phrase he used of Buddhism, Christianity &c.), Quaternary, Hominid invention for crudely pacifying the purely physiological characteristic of Hominid cephalic capacity. He viewed the concept of theism as cowardly, conceited, unimaginative and, necessarily, at the *earliest* merely Pliocene. (His period was Precambrian, before god.)

His irascibility increased towards the end...

[Missionaries visited him clutching 'Good News' bibles.] You are importunate. Return to your corrugated-iron chapels and crave forgiveness of your wretched deity for disturbing the lucubrations of a bad hat.

* * *

It is a most terrible *bore*
to haemorrhage, spewing up gore,
and, bubbling for breath,
be blood-drowned to death.
Je *ne* voudrais *pas* être mort.

You find the Limerick inapposite? Care for a cutely-adapted Adonic?

After he spewed up
he was unconscious
till about tea-time,
when he woke up, then
vomited once more
(blood and fish-smelling
purplish matter).
Then he said 'Darling,
please do not leave me,
I think I'm –' nothing
else. He slumped heavy,
staining my clothing
puce and burnt-umber
(drying black later).
He was my husband –
we had been married
25 good years.

* * *

In ornithological days, at the observatory, we used, not infrequently, to discover moribund specimens. They seemed always to have grovelled into some niche to quietly get on with it – the stance would so often be trembling on a single weak leg, the lids half-closed, the grey nictitating membrane half-drawn across the, by then, dull bead. Several species, on dissection, revealed carcinomatic infestation.

The use of narcotics, dehydration and breathing through the mouth have led to his mouth becoming troublesome. We prepare, in our pharmacy, an artificial saliva containing methyl-cellulose and glycerin which eases thirst and dry mouth.

* * *

[His wife and daughter tend him at home, bewildered by this revelation of his, of *all,* frailty. Special Laundry Services deal with his sheets and blankets – the soiling too foul for acceptance by normal laundries. The ambulance's arrival would be as the tumbrel's.]

Briskly efficiently deftly my daughter enters at midnight,
eases me onto my side, changes the oxygen flask.

Even formed properly, no elegiac distich can fall with
quite this sospirity: breath – out of a black mask exhaled.

None of it matters except at a purely personal level:
pain, not oblivion, hurts; as with me, so with all quarks.

* * *

The specialist's hands, extremely large, buff-coloured, gently manipulate my emaciated wrist, two slender bones and a knot of turquoise vein. Huge tawny thumb and forefinger tighten on a frail pulse.

It was a good ferret and almost immediately there was a rabbit in the net. The man I was with (a gyppo-looking type whose company I cultivated as a child but whose name evades me now) removed it from the nylon mesh. His hands were huge and tawny and took up the rabbit, smoothing its ruffled fur, and with soothing fondness, with infinite gentleness, affectionately snapped its neck.

* * *

'His questions were probably mere pleas for reassurance. I did not tell him. I seldom tell them. Some of my colleagues disagree; many are of the same opinion as myself. According to Oken ("What to tell cancer patients", *Journal of the American Medical Association*, 1961, *175*, p.1120), about 80% of us rarely, if ever, tell them.'

According to Gilbertsen and Wangensteen ('Should the doctor tell the patient the disease is cancer?', in *The Physician and the Total Care of the Cancer Patient*, American Cancer Society, New York, 1961), about 80% of patients say they would like to be told.

* * *

I am told that I was rude to a folk-singer who 'writes his own material' (of the You'll-Always-Be-On-My-Mind-Girl/Nuclear-Holocaust-Is-An-Awful-Shame School). He had, at his own considerable expense, caused a record of his ghastly outpourings to be manufactured. He solicited me to buy one. I declined. 'Why?' 'Because I believe you to be devoid of talent, mawkish and platitudinous.' (Sniffily) 'I'm not going to stay here and be insulted.' He went. It was as if one had flicked a smut from one's lapel.

* * *

'Quite the most maudlin man I've ever met
told me this in the lounge of the Colliers:
"It's many years ago now but, oh God!,
I can still feel her hand rubbing my tool
as she drove slowly down the pleached-hedged lane.
She stopped the car, licked her lips, moaned, and kissed me –

Christ!, slurping tongues like squirming warm oiled slugs –
and said 'God!, I could eat you' and unzipped
my washed-out Levi's, peeled them apart and guzzled.
I'll never see her again – I've got bowel cancer." '
Run them together, set as justified prose
the inadequately blank pentameters.

* * *

Now for a bit of a trip down Memory Lane. Spring breakfast, bluebells on sun-dappled gingham. A blue-hooped jug of cream, bronzed toast, Frank Cooper's. Smoked aromatic crepitating rashers. FREE!!! IN EACH PACK OF *BRAN-BREK* – A PLASTIC BUG!!! I am served a dusty handful, read the packet. *Medical Scientists are in agreement. We all need fibre, and bran is full of fibre. BRAN-BREK is full of bran, so eat BRAN-BREK. Doctors say fibreless diets cause bowel cancer. Don't take the risk – get into the BRAN-BREK habit.* What was then fear has become shitless ˙terror.

* * *

Have you ever been in one of them? They really are depressing. Anyway, we were visiting someone – actually, the husband's mother it was, and the kid was with us so it all rather comes home to you that in a few years that'll be *you* in that bed and the kid, grown up, with *its* kid, visiting *you*... Anyway, in the next bed was this, you can only call it 'thing', – no bedclothes, just an official nightdress thing – and while we were telling lies to *our* one, it started up a sort of whining gurgling wheezing noise. [**To be continued.**]

* * *

[**Contd.**] I tried to crack on I hadn't noticed anything, but it kept on and on and I saw it was trying to attract my attention so I couldn't do anything but try to savvy what it was on about. It couldn't move, except sort of rock its head and flap one arm against its side. And all the time that queer noise. Its mouth wouldn't close and whenever it made that noise 'Waahg waahgrrglz' spittle with streaks of red dribbled out. It turned out that it wanted the screens pulled round it, and *I* had to do it. *Uuuugh!*

* * *

I seen him once before, before – you know. I was fetching a white Welsh, 12 hands, down Grindle Nills. Between Grindle Hollow and Oakleymill there was him and his Mrs and nipper. Picnicking, they was, wine cooling in the brook. He gawped at the nag's pricked ears, large eye, dished profile, withers, mane, poll, forelock, muzzle, chin, cheek, shoulder, chest, forearm, knee, cannon, pastern, chestnut, brisket, elbow, belly, stifle, gaskin, coronet, wall of hoof, heel, fetlock, hock, thigh, buttock, dock, croup, loins, back. He knew who I was all right. 'That's a pale one ye have there, Mr Tucker' he said.

* * *

At the end of the Cambrian, an-estimated 52% of faunal families became extinct. At the end of the Devonian, 30%. At the end of the Permian, 50%. At the end of the Triassic, 35%. At the end of the Cretacious, 26%. Last night I had to get up frequently and stagger to the bathroom at the end of the ward. Pain unendurable. Rocked back and forth on lavatory seat, groaning. At the end of the Holocene (fashionable Tropical Rain Forest reduction, fashionable Nuclear Holocaust) the percentage of faunal family extinction is likely to at least compare with Cambrian figures.

* * *

[He writes] *Dear* [names of his wife and child which I render 'A' and 'B' for reasons of delicacy], *I recall our Callow Hollow alfresco. Our tiny child bathing in Oakleymill Waterfall pool. A gorse sprig suspended in an eddy. We were at the best of our lives. Such happiness never recurs. Ever. Golden bright little flower, sharp thorns. Spätlese cooling in the gelid spring. Later, the gipsy with that pale gelding. I will remember these things until the day I die.* [Which is the day after tomorrow. He signs his name which I render 'C' for reasons of delicacy.]

* * *

'Retention can give rise to undue pain;/incontinence, conversely, causes shame/and a degree of inconvenience./ Colostomies, short-circuiting the bowel/to open on the frontal abdomen,/can cause distress at first, but nothing like/the anguish that the blockage, not relieved,/would cause. Soon after surgery, it seems,/ some soiling from the new colostomy/is unavoidable – patients become/aware that they can get unclean and smell...'

Terminal verse. Rain-pits 700000000 years old in Precambrian rock: a species evolved 696000000 years after that: a handful of stresses and punctuation: ars only as long as vita: pentameters, like colons, inadequate.

* * *

100 days after diagnosis, I ingest soporifics. I compose octave and first line of sestet concerning my cadaver.

> The vagrant Tucker found it, partly rotted,
> Eyes gouged by corvids, puffed blue meat, wet, stinking,
> Blown lips serrated (nibbled as if pinking-
> Shears had been at them), maggoty nose besnotted.
> From its arse pocket he took five green-spotted
> (With *Penicillia*) £5 notes – thinking,
> Quite rightly, they'd be better used for drinking
> Bass in The Whale than festering, rank, clotted
>
> In (something something something) Ashes Hollow

Why? snot, gore, filth, suppuration of the arse-gut – for these *no* metric is vindicable.

* * *

A regular at the Colliers was Head of Art at the local Poly (phoney smoothie, used to take snuff). Mort bought some Itchy Powder from the Wizard's Den Joke Shop and one evening, when the Art bloke offered the old silver snuff-box round the bar, our hero slipped the irritant in (looked just like snuff) and handed back the antique. The offensive educationalist took no more stimulant until, on the motorway, driving back home, he indulged, and, in the paroxysm of sneezing that ensued, collided with an oncoming articulated lorry hauling meat-and-bone-meal and was killed instantly.

* * *

In the Borough Library the medical dictionaries are mostly used by unfortunates looking up their maladies. The Cs are particularly well-thumbed. CARCINAEMIA CARCINECTOMY CARCINELCOSIS CARCINOGEN CARCINOGENESIS CARCINOGENIC CARCINOGENICITY CARCINOID CARCINOLOGY CARCINOLYSIN CARCINOLYSIS CARCIN-OLYTIC CARCINOMATOID CARCINOMATOPHOBIA CARCINOMATOSIS CARCINOMATOUS CARCINOMECTOMY CARCINOMELCOSIS CAR-CINOPHILIA CARCINOPHILIC CARCINOPHOBIA CARCINOSARCOMA CARCINOSECTOMY CARCINOSIS CARCINOSTATIC CARCINOUS. I am researching **C. ventriculi**; the woman who has just relinquished Stedman's has marked faintly in pencil **C. of uterine cervix**. We are beyond verse here. No one wants to write 'On Last Looking Into Stedman's Carcinoma'. Nevertheless, I have invented the 13-line sonnet for unlucky people (100 words, inc. title)...

* * *

Talking Shop

The three sterilisations went OK,
except for the advanced C. uterine cervix
(just my damned luck to find that) – anyway,
apart from that it all went normally.
The one in Number 2 was staggered when
I said 'We found your coil, by the way –
worked its way through the womb into the space
between the womb and stomach.' Number 3
(non compos mentis, got eight kids already)
asked me when 'it' would be all right again.
I said 'If you endeavour to avoid
sexual intercourse for about two nights...'
She said 'He won't wait. He *will* have his rights.'

* * *

The sham the twee and the precious/phoney-rustic ignorant/ wield their sugary Biros/down in the safe Sticks/ensconced in the done-up Old Wheelwright's./Poetical mawkish duff gen/ where a buzzard is 'noble' and lands/in a tree (surprise, surprise!)/to corroborate some trite tenet/cum badly-observed Nature Note./ Their fauna is furry or feathery/people like you and me,/cute or nasty – a raptor/becomes a Belfast terrorist./ Bullshit bullshit bullshit/of the Plashy Fen School./Peterson, Mountfort & Hollom/write more sense than you/bloody carpetbaggers.

* * *

According to Parkes ('Bereavement and mental illness', *British Journal of Medical Psychology*, 1965, *38*, p.1), 8% of seriously distressed bereaved people questioned expressed anger towards the dead person.

'She didn't seem particularly distraught. We were just with her at the ceremony. Suddenly she just seemed to ignore us all. "Why have you left me, why have you gone away? Why have you left me, why have you gone away? Why have you left me, why have you gone away? Why have you left me, why have you gone away?" She yelled and yelled as it went into the furnace.'

* * *

Muse! Sing *Phylloscopus trochiloides!*/I know it is a strange thing to recall/out of a rag-bag of experience/(rather than, say, rude goings-on with girls/or that first fright of Death – lost in thick fog/and with the tide coming in rapidly/over the mud-flats in the river mouth...),/but, more than early childhood or first dick,/ this vagrant (which I mist-netted in youth)/incongruously gladdens my last thoughts / (and, more incongruous still, in quatorzain). / The wing formula confirmed that it was Greenish/(rather than Arctic) Warbler – longer first/and shorter second primary, of course.

* * *

We went to picnic up Calo Holow to have a picnic to a wortofall and a pool the pool was very deep. I neely fell into the pool. it was very suney We had cold chicin. Daddy and Mummy lay in the gras by the streem and I played round about and had oranj juse then Mummy and daddy had some wine that was cooling in the streem. Here is a powim of it

> When I went up Calo Hill
> I took some orang I did not spill.
>
> we saw a pale grey poniy
> Daddy fel asleep by the streem

* * *

It's bad for us as well, you know, looking after them. Can you take any more? I can't. I'm ready to give up. What's the use? All our patients die eventually. They should do six things for their 'Death Work': (1) become aware of their impending death, (2) balance hope and fear throughout the crisis, (3) *reverse* physical survival instincts, (4) relinquish independence, (5) detach themselves from former experiences and (6) prepare 'spiritually' for death. They go through six emotional states (outlined by Kübler Ross): (1) Denial, (2) Isolation, (3) Anger, (4) Bargaining, (5) Depression, (6) Acceptance. All, eventually. All.

* * *

These are the sorts of things they say, through six emotional states (outlined by Kübler-Ross), sad, self-deceiving till the last ones: 'It's just one of those things' 'I shall be out of here soon' 'I'm getting better' 'I'm feeling fine' 'It's not so bad' 'I just need a good tonic' 'Be back at work before you can say "Jack Robinson"' 'My pneumonia's worse than my cancer'. Can you take any more? I can't. I'm ready to give up. What's the use? All our patients die eventually. Anyway, those are the things they first say, DENIAL. Next comes ISOLATION:

* * *

'You don't know how it feels' 'You can't know how it feels' 'No one understands' 'They don't tell you anything' 'I try to guess what's going on' 'On your morning rounds you seem too busy to talk' 'No one seems to realise how vital my supply of oxygen is' 'I try to hide my feelings so that the family's not too distressed' 'Don't like being on my own' 'I don't like being left alone'. Those who we have not told start to sense it – the way the nurses look at them, the way we see less and less of them...

* * *

Next comes ANGER: 'Why *me*?' 'They don't care' 'It's my body they treat you like a child of 3' 'The food's lousy' 'The Quack's no good' 'A God of Love – huh!' 'The nurses is lazy' 'Why don't this happen to the scroungers and layabouts?' 'Doctor's a fool if he thinks this treatment will work'. Next comes BARGAINING: 'If only I could be home for the daughter's wedding, I'd not care after that' 'If only I could go without pain, I wouldn't mind so much' 'If only God would spare me to do His work a little longer, wouldn't mind then'.

* * *

Can you take any more? I can't. I'm ready to give up. What's the use? All our patients die eventually. By now they can no longer depend on their bodies doing what, before they got ill, they thought they would do in such an eventuality – neither suicide, nor smart philosophising. They can not conceive beforehand what it will be like. Dying nobly? My sweet arse hole. One of them wrote verse. Verse! Write verse about this: a Left Inguinal Colostomy. Shit, blood, puke and a body no longer dependable, metastases, dyspnoea ... I shut my eyes but weep under the lids.

* * *

The fifth emotional state (outlined by Kübler-Ross) is that of DEPRESSION: 'What chance have I got?' 'Not long now' 'What's the use?' 'This cancer is the end of everything' 'I'm not going to get better' 'I'm so useless now'. Last comes ACCEPTANCE: 'Thank you for all you've done' 'Dying will be a relief' 'I see things differently now' 'The wife will be so terribly lost and lonely'. These are the sorts of things they say through the six emotional states (outlined by Kübler-Ross), sad, self-deceiving till the last ones. It's bad for us as well, you know.

* * *

I ndian doctor examines
N ewly performed colotomy (is appalled).

3

T erminal case, brought into
H ere last night, won't
E ver return to Azalea Terrace.

2

S mall frightened old woman,
A fter anaesthetic, has dim
M emory of fainting in chip-shop (won't
E ver get out of here).

1

V ery smooth-looking
E xecutive-type in
R oad accident; surgeons
T ry to revive him, fail;
I n collison with lorry
C arrying meat-and-bone-meal.
A n elderly lady, supposed suicidal,
L oudly denies taking barbiturates.

G

C oke is shovelled
O nto the furnace by a
L oathsome old stoker who now
U nfolds the Sports Page,
M arks with an X some
N ag for the next Meeting.

B

292

Mort or *Char* (this latter pronounced 'chair' or 'care' in their infernal accents, though, presumably, merely short for Charlie) possesses many katabolic anecdotes. His erstwhile leman bestowed fingernail and teeth impressions on the mantelpiece as her distemper flourished and the burden of pain induced gripping and biting the mahogany often for hours together in the full excruciating anguish of the paroxysm. The huge firm 18-year-old malleable boobs she had let him enjoy were defiled at 42 by surgeon's scalpel and radium treatment. This, rendered into catalectic tetrameters, might do for the *TLS* or other reputable literary periodical.

* * *

What were bronzed on Margate sands,
flopped about by trembling hands,
malleable, conical,
have become ironical.
What was cupped in palm and thumb
seres now under radium.
What was kneaded like warm dough
is where, now, malign cells grow.
What was fondled in a car
through white silk-smooth slippery bra
(Marks & Spencer, 38)
was plump cancer inchoate.

Truncation (catalexis): 'frequent in trochaic verse, where the line of complete trochaic feet tends to create monotony. The following trochaic lines exhibit t.: "Simple maiden, void of art, / Babbling out the very heart"...' – *Princeton Encyclopedia of Poetry and Poetics* (ed. Preminger).

* * *

He speaks to me and doodles the disorder's initial letter with green Biro in his desk-diary. Croissant? Banana? Sickle blade? He is frightened of what I will ask. Some of them will not tell you, nor prescribe what you really need. Perhaps an accumulation from a bogus insomnia claim, then, after the magnum of '61 *Cheval Blanc*, end with the 19th century Bual before taking them. Stylish finish, with the fine initialled decanter. Green discharge smothers the hideous curve, enormous now, and a suppurating colon punctuates it. I can almost scent the *Cheval Blanc* as I think of it.

* * *

when she first found it feel this she said oh god it can't be can it lump probably nothing he said better just x-ray be on safe side swarming teeming oh god if could turn back calendar only a few pages she went bald radium god pain bald horrible years ago on the Med when she god they were magnificent huge golden tanned god bald·like a skull hugest on the beach

[Cold truncating surgeon's blade
razes what was St Tropezed.

Tomorrow she will occupy the 2nd floor Infirmary bed where now a patient from Azalea Terrace is expiring.]

* * *

'The husband was driving. The wife, aged 23, was in the back seat. They were on the motorway. She had just been discharged from a mental institution. Without comment she took 20 barbiturates. Suddenly the young man became aware that she was comatose on the sheepskin cover. He observed the empty brown plastic phial. In panic he screeched into a Services Area and – ' 'Why had she tried to, you know?' 'Terrible fear of getting cancer, no reason to suspect it, just kept thinking she would.' (Great unvindicable idea: a 17-liner, 100-word, pentameter acrostic, first letters forming *CARCINOMATOPHOBIA*.) 'Continue.'

* * *

'He carried her into the Ladies' Lavatory intending to make her puke up the offending drug. She could not be made to vomit. An elderly lady, unable to enter the lavatory because it was thus occupied, sat on a chair outside the cubicle. Frenzied, the young husband raced to telephone for an ambulance, leaving his spouse unconscious in the toilet. He dialled 999 on the Cafeteria phone. The Cafeteria Manageress forced him to consume three cups of hot sweet tea. Meanwhile, ambulancemen arrived, accused the seated elderly lady of ingesting barbiturates, and, despite her protestations, bore her away by stretcher.'

* * *

Constantly anticipating cancer/(Abdominal, lung, throat, breast, uterus,/Rectum, 'malevolent' or 'benign'), she went/Crackers and was soon certifiable./Inside, the loopiest of all was the/Nutdoctor who prescribed barbiturates/'Only as soporifics – one per night'./ Months passed, and she accumulated 20./At length she was discharged. Her husband called/To chauffeur her. 'Apparently depressed/Or meditative, otherwise OK,/Perhaps a change of scene?...' Motoring back,/Hopelessly fraught, she polished off the lot./Overdose verdict brought by coroner.../Bloody fool ambulance-wallahs kidnapped some/Idle bystander (who they thought looked ill)/And left the suicide slumped in the bogs.

* * *

Ubi sunt the blue-green algae of yesteryear that by photosynthesis first oxygenated the atmosphere? In the black cherts of the Bulawayan Limestone Group dated at about three thousand one hundred million years old, in the stromatolitic sediments first noted by Macgregor, later corroborated by Schopf et al; that is where. *Ubi sunt* the good old rain-pits and ripple-marks so transiently formed about six hundred million years ago? Buried in the Late Precambrian Longmyndian matrices of this valley where I myself... What is 40 years here or there on the chronostratigraph? (They don't make them like that anymore.)

* * *

When I worked with Schopf, on the Bulawayan stromatolites, I took twelve specimens of the limestone, each having a maximum dimension of 15 cm and exhibiting one or more areas of iron-stained, crescentic laminations of weathered surfaces. The best of these exhibited seven areas of lamination on the external surfaces and I gently broke it along the planes of weakness perpendicular to the laminations, exposing five additional laminated areas. I photographed the broken fragments and prepared a plaster cast of each. Those laminates were 3100000000 years old; I am dying (Carcinoma ventriculi) but the Holocene is of scant importance.

* * *

Ubi sunt J. William Schopf, Dorothy Z. Oehler, Robert J. Horodyski and Keith A. Kvenvolden, whose 'Biogenicity and Significance of the Oldest Known Stromatolites' (*Journal of Paleontology*, Vol. 45, No. 3, pp. 477-485) so inspired us? They are now one with the cold stromatolitic limestone and laminated carbonaceous cherts of the Huntsman Limestone Quarries near Turk Mine, 55 km north-north-east of Bulawayo; that is where. *Ubi sunt* God? and pusill-animous Nietzsche (who merely substituted Übermenschen)? Sedimented. *Ubi sunt* Übermenschen? and the Master of the 100 100-Word Units? Sedimented, sedimented. (They don't make them like that anymore.)

* * *

'They are angry with their own failing bodies...also apt to criticise and blame others...One such aggrieved...greatly troubled the nurses and doctors who cared for her... Often young nurses would leave her bedside to shed a few tears because their attempts to help her had been met by contemptuous dismissal ... accusing those who were treating her of apathy inefficiency and callousness...a way of expressing her disappointment and bitterness...for herself and the life that seemed unfulfilled...' – John Hinton, *Dying*, (Penguin, 1967).

His irascibility increased towards the end...

'Piss off, Sky Pilot,' I whisper in the Padre's ear.

* * *

Sky cerulean. Sheep-cropped moist short sprung bright green turf where I lie, face up, my head on a stone at the brook edge. Upstream a metre and downstream a metre, trickling sound registers in each ear, an alto tinkling, a basso gurgling, the upper notes resembling skylark song, the lower resembling bathwater unplugged, concurrently continuously varying. My bare arms warm in bright sun. My husband beside me, touches. Suddenly our young daughter hugs me, hugs me again. Gewürztraminer rocks in the cool current. Cold roasted partridges in a white linen towel. Late autumn, but, something irrevocably ~~pleasant~~ has occurred.

lovely

* * *

My ward, 1A, was called Harley Ward (after the famous street, I assume). On arrival I was led into a tiny office to fill in forms which included questions like 'Have you been living in the UK for more than 12 months?' and 'Have your mother and father been living in the UK for more than 12 months?' Then I was labelled: a plastic strap was snapped round my wrist and inside its waterproof sheath was my name and number and what I was in for – colotomy. This perhaps reduces the likelihood of some innocent part being removed by mistake.

* * *

(Not just me, but all of us in the same vertical column. I pass the same hopeless pyjamad cases in ghastly contraptions daily. In the snot-green corridors daily the covered trolleys are shunted. Daily the meat-waggons swing through the gates braying, pulsing blue light, their burdens already history scraped off the Tarmac. Daily and nightly the trolleys the trolleys the trolleys jingle like gently shaken tambourines as they hasten with cargoes of shiny stainless-steel kidney-shaped bowls and glinting clamps, needles and blades and forceps, acres of soft white lint to one or another and finally all.)

* * *

Then I was led to my bed and shown my locker. I was to undress, stow away my clothes and lie down. A nurse curtained me off from the others. She recorded my temperature and pulse, took my blood pressure and shaved me with an old razor across the stomach from the navel down, removing about an inch of pubic hair. Then I produced a urine sample in a bed pan. After that there was nothing to do until the anaesthetist was due to see me at 5 pm. I produced my *Times* which was stolen by a marauding nurse.

* * *

The doctor had told me but not him. One evening he was struggling with a pile of papers – administrative stuff, to do with the conference on Early Precambrian Stromatolite Morphology and Taxonomy – when he slumped into his seat, exhausted by the simple exertion. I touched his arm and said (I hear my voice and its slight echo from the sparsely furnished study as if it is played back to me on tape) 'Oh my darling, you should not trouble with anything unessential; you see, you are dying.' He simply replied 'I understand' and replaced the documents in the mahogany bureau.

* * *

Radio 2 blared over a loudspeaker system. There was a radio with earphones behind my bed, so I tried to tune in to something else. There was a dial which read RADIO-1 RADIO-2 RADIO-3 RADIO-4. I clicked the indicator around the dial through three-hundred-and-sixty degrees. Radio 2 was vigorously transmitted at every calibration on the instrument. A trolley was driven at me by a gentleman with dirty fingernails. This vehicle supported a large urn of grey tea and a material bearing the legend BRAN SPONGE, BY THE MAKERS OF BRAN-BREK. I declined.

* * *

(Not just me, but out there in the Pedestrianised Precincts. The filth gathers beyond clearance or control. In gales the crisp yellow newspapers soar above the high-rises and out to sea or lodge in electric wires or pile up against shop doors. New desolate sounds of Coke cans discarded tinkling rolling in windy streets over greasy flags, and cables slapped clacking against tin masts of yachts in deserted lidos. In Department Stores staff outnumber customers now. The Cosmetics assistants, painted like Archie Andrews, look frightened at scant trade. In Furnishings, Glassware, Heel Bar, Carpeting...something irrevocably dying is happening.)

* * *

The anaesthetist arrived, tampered with my heart and lungs, felt all round the ribs and implored me to breathe deeply while he listened. My blood pressure was up. He seemed desirous I should sleep and prescribed a soporific. I should be given a pre-med injection in the thigh about 2 pm on Tuesday and about 3 pm be taken into the Recovery Room and injected in the back of the hand to 'knock me out completely'. He'd 'bring me round' again and I'd be trundled back to bed. Incongruously, he inspected my fingernails. No doubt he found them charming.

* * *

Newsflash, their women writhe unconsolable in the dirt of Ulster and the Holy Land. They are not actresses; that is how they really feel. How I feel also, my cancerous husband. Newsflash after newsflash, their women writhe unconsolable in the dirt of Ulster and the Holy Land. They are not actresses; that is how they really feel. How I feel also, my cancerous husband. Newsflash after newsflash after stinking newsflash, their women writhe unconsolable in the dirt of Ulster and the Holy Land. They are not actresses; that is how they really feel. How I feel also, my cancerous husband.

* * *

I was fed Health Authority Chicken Supreme and semolina and jam and made to watch television where a woman turned into a spider during the full-moon, hunted respectable citizens, injected them with poison, swathed them in web cocoons and carried them off to her Transylvanian silo. I was given Ovaltine and sleeping-draught and endured insomnia all night. On Tuesday I was given tea at 6 am. 'Have you "performed"?' 'What do you mean?' I was given a suppository and told to keep it in for 20 minutes. I got cramp up the arse and shat after 5 minutes.

* * *

(Not just me, but the public clocks in the cities are fucked-up – / the Building Society one, the one on the Bank,/the one on the Town Hall, the one at the Station, all stopped/at a hopeless time and, whereas when I was a child/they were constants to be relied on, now the resources/and requisite knowledge to fix them are gone. And this isn't/some crusty superannuated old Colonel/ lamenting, saying 'Of course, it was all fields then...',/but me, as my cardio-whatsit ticks limply, observing/the clocks all knackered, whereas they used not to be.)

* * *

I have invented
a brand new kind of sonnet
where the octave is
a tanka plus a haiku
and the sestet two haikus.
But is there, today,
one ghastly experience
that vindicates verse?

Outside the chip-shop
an ambulance's blue light
throbs at heartbeat rate.
Someone has dropped dead;
tidily weighed syllables
drip from the draped stiff.

Why *verse?* At PRIDE OF PLAICE, the chippy opposite the Leisure
Centre, a horrible old human is slouched with its head cradled in
the alarmed proprietor's arms. Nearby a beggar swigs White Horse,
grey abrasive palm like a parched tongue anticipating small coin.

* * *

Char helped the Undertaker once. The passenger had lived alone
in a cottage with a couple of dogs. It sat rigid in an armchair, sap-
green translucent glaze over the cheekbones. Char smoothed the
back of his finger gently over the brow (the skin was unpliable, cool,
waxen) then leered, and between thumb and grimy palm grasped
the yellow lardy chin and shook it with hatred. The grey tongue
lolled. One of the dogs, a trembling whippet, mounted the cadaver's
bare knee, ejaculating after several minutes' rut. Char pocketed £25
from the mantelpiece, lowered the stiff into its fibreglass vessel.

* * *

Breakfast at 8 am was toast and tea. This was to be my last food for 24 hours. At 11 am I had a Savlon bath. I was given a sachet of concentrated disinfectant to put in the water and told to immerse to the ears and wash the face in it. I was put in surgical robes of crisp white linen and a gauze cap and returned to bed. I waited thus absurdly for the anaesthetist. Radio 2 was statutory. The first injection was 'in the bottom to gently relax you'. I scrutinised the ceiling for signs of change.

* * *

When I worked with Schopf on the Huntsman Quarry stromatolites, we concluded that the Bulawayan deposit could be interpreted as placing a minimum age (*ca* 3100000000 yrs) on the origin of cyanophycean algae, of the filamentous habit, and of integrated biological communities of procaryotic micro-organisms presumably including producers (blue-green algae), reducers (aerobic and anaerobic bacteria) and consumers (bacteria, predatory by absorption). This interpretation was supported by the occurrence of filamentous and unicellular algalike and bacterium-like microfossils in other Early Precambrian sediments. I am dying (Carcinoma ventriculi) but what is 40 years here or there on the chronostratigraph?

* * *

Everything became pellucid. I seemed on the brink of some revelation or original idea. Then I ceased to focus and my eyelids felt heavy. I think I dozed because the time went very quickly. A Romany-looking stretcher-bearer shuttled to and fro. I couldn't establish what he did with his poles. The stretchers were canvas. A trolley would come in. He inserted his poles. A patient was eased into bed. The poles were removed. I could not see what he did with the poles. I became irascible. I wanted to demand testily of him 'Account for your poles, sir!'

* * *

302

I should have started my sabbatical
but now it is impossible. Six weeks
ago they took the part-time employee,
hired to replace me, into hospital,
opened him up and said he had three months
before he pegged out – cancerous guts. They fetched
some out, but found too much inside.

                                        He keeps
a sort of journal, so they say, in which
he chronicles his death in the 3rd Person,
partly in prose, part verse, peculiar, hey?
He's only youngish too. So that's the end
of my sabbatical – I'm pretty miffed
(nor, I suppose, is he too chuffed about it).

                    *   *   *

I helped myself onto the stretcher. I was wheeled through the
double doors into a bathroom-green room. The anaesthetist slapped
my hand to raise a vein. 'You'll feel a small prick and a little scratch.
There. Now it should be beginning to take effect.' I tried to say
yes but said yuriuree. 'You may be feeling a cold sensation.' Yura-
yuaress. A masked nurse in green said 'Can you see me? Can you
focus on my face?' I tried to say yes but couldn't. I tried to say
wind but said wiznera ah. She raised my head and I farted.

                    *   *   *

No verse is | adequate. || Most of us | in this ward
will not get | out again. || This poor sod | next to me
will be dead | in a month. || He is young, | has not been
married long, | is afraid || (so am I, | so am I).
When his wife | visits him || (every day, | every day)
he takes hold | of her sleeve, || clutches her | savagely
screaming 'Please, | get me well! || Dear sweet God, | make me well!'
Quasi sham | tétramètre, || sub Corneille, | sub Racine,
is too grand, | is too weak, || for this slow | tragedy,
screaming 'Please, | get me well! || Dear sweet God, | make me well!'

                    *   *   *

Wheeled back to bed. I try to lift my arms. Cannot. The Romany performs with his mysterious poles. I am told to get some sleep. Staff Nurse calls the stretcher-blankets 'cuddlies'. Throat rusk-dry. I am uncomfortable but unable to turn onto my side. Eventually I heave myself onto my side...At an unknown time tea is brought. I feel sick. They wash my face and hands. The rubber under the sheets makes me sweat. BRAN-BREK is proffered. The surgeon who performed it appears. A pleasant, worried Sikh. He is afraid of what I am going to ask.

* * *

(Not just me, but also, out there, the cities whose shit/surges into the sea in tsunamis,/and Shopping Precincts whose shit of canines and rolling/Coke tins and paper and fag-ends and polystyrene/chip-trays and plastic chip-forks rattle in bleak winds,/and those who wash least, breed most, to all of us, all,/a shoddy incontrovertible burial in shit./

This isn't some crusty Colonel (retired) lamenting/'Of course it was all fields then, you see, in those days...',/but me, me, suppurating to death,/not just on my own but with us all, with us all.)

* * *

Ubi sunt Chaloner ALABASTER, Guido BACH, William CADGE, William Otto Adolph Julius DANCKWERTS, His Excellency Dr Johannes Friedrich August von ESMARCH, His Honour Judge William Wynne FFOULKES, Sydney GRUNDY, Henry HOOK, Eugene Clutterbuck IMPEY, James JOICEY, Nesbitt KIRCHHOFFER, Chih Chen LO FENG-LUH, Budgett MEAKIN, Alfred Trubner NUTT, John Orlando Hercules Norman OLIVER, Mrs PUDDI-COMBE, Harry QUILTER, Rt. Hon. Sir Horace RUMBOLD, John SPROT, Gaspard le Marchant TUPPER, Emanual Maguire UNDER-DOWN, Thomas Henry Bourke VADE-WALPOLE, Edward Montagu Granville Montagu Stuart Wortley Mackenzie WHARNCLIFFE, His Honour Judge Lawford YATE-LEE, Guiseppe ZANARDELLI? (In *Who Was Who 1897-1915*, that's where.)

* * *

Some of us benefit from a self-shielding shunning of awful
thoughts about dying and, worse, physical pain at the end.

Nevertheless we are conscious of being falsely deluding,
when we say jauntily 'Oh! I shall be out of here soon!'

Adequate realisation of what is truly awaiting
does not prevent us from this: never admitting we *know*.

Even though sometimes I talk about this abdominal cancer,
my mental ease demands lies, comfort of make-believe games –

such as this one that I play now in distich, almost pretending
verse has validity. No. Verse is fuck-all use here, now.

* * *

The meat-waggon comes for another unfortunate. Borne out of
Azalea Terrace, the disgusting old victim looks glum, stunned,
stupid, no longer working properly. There is bright pink spit drib-
bling onto the clean black sleeve of an ambulance man who holds
one end of a stainless steel wheelchair thing and cradles the nasty
head. Cold metallic joints lock slickly. A disinfectant whiff. One-
way window. Blue pulse. Sitting on a yellow fibreglass road-grit
bunker, the Mad Tramp pulls at a whisky bottle (White Horse)
and guffaws a perfect pentameter:

Hă há | hă há | hă há | hă há | hă há.

* * *

Evolution (including mass faunal extinction, at the end of the Cambrian, Holocene &c.) is what happens – not what *should*, according to *sapiens* interpretations, happen.

It seems to be the greatest pain I've known in my life. Respiration fails because of it, sweat streams, I think (I *hope*) I'll faint under it. Members of hospital staff are conditioned to pay no heed to (nor administer sufficient analgesics for) such excruciation. I feel mental as well as physical strain and inadequacy.

None of it *matters* (except at a purely personal level). Pain, not oblivion, hurts. As with me, so with all quarks.

* * *

[He breaks down and sobs embarrassingly.] Oh! I shall miss you so. Why has it happened? Why has stuff inside me suddenly gone terribly wrong? I don't think I'm afraid of not *being* anymore but so terribly terribly frightened of not being *with you*. And the child; no more playing catch with that large red-and-blue-spotted plastic ball. Never. Anymore. She called it Mr Spotty. [Mawkish drivel.] I can't be brave tonight. Oh my darling, help me! Look after me! Can't be brave or consoled by philosophy or by po – would willingly never have written anything if *only*

* * *

He had just died and screens surrounded the bed but the porter had not had opportunity to remove the body. I arrived at Visiting Hour when all the nurses were busy and unable to intercept me. I went straight to the screened bed and, employing a funny voice (derived from Donald Duck) which we had developed during our years of marriage for times of particular playfulness, addressed the occupant through the plastic panel thus: 'Howsqush my dearsqsh old drake thisqush eveningsqush?'. Visitors at adjacent beds regarded me patronisingly. Then I bobbed my head round the screen and confronted the shroud.

* * *

[He writes] *Darling* [names of wife and daughter] *won't last (too weak)*
till Visiting Hour. Hope you find this. Last notes. Biro on Kleenex,
fitting medium terminal words. Oh! Oh weep for Adonais he is dead. C3:
the lowest grade of physical fitness in Military Service. On the filthy
window-ledge of this ward a foul cleg in a patina of grease and dust
whizzes around and around and. The only way to cross the Acheron is
on inflated egos. Sleep after toil port after stormy seas, Ease after war,
death after life does greatly please. Two last Spenserians? [Pah.]

* * *

Interdenominational claptrap,
from the Infirmary Chaplains, helps a few
cowardly of us bear our deaths. The chap
whom they leucotomised conceives this true:
that his soul is eternal. Such a view,
wholly unsatisfactory for me,
is genuinely good – he won't pull through,
but hopes to die without finality
accepting their dud-specious immortality.

Other poltroons amongst us, though, are scared
not of not *being* any more, but just
of terminal agony, are unprepared
[311. of MS. lacking ....
....
....]
Still more of us fear pain *and* being dust,
and for us nothing can (nor god, nor soul,
nor analgesic, nor philosophy) console.

* * *

It started with his urinating blood. We looked at it in the lavatory pan and were terrified. He went to morning surgery. He had to go for tests. They found he had a bladder carcinoma, little mushroomy things – we saw a photo. They forced something into him through a tube stuck into his penis hole. After the op they kept the tube in for a long time. It caused him to have a hard-on all the time it was in. He was in pain. He had to have regular check-ups. It seemed clear for ages, but recurred, *massively*.

* * *

[He breaks down and sobs embarrassingly.] I keep thinking *if only*. Oh, help me! And I can't believe it – that I am really going to   It is as if I were just writing about someone else d – just as if it were yet another of the things about those poor *other* people that I write (*used to* write) about. Why am I writing about it? Can't be brave tonight. [Drivel.] Oh, my darling, if only I could stay here not go not go not die! [Drivel.] Oh, I shall miss you so [Drivel.] terribly! terribly! Oh my dear darl [&c.]

* * *

Of course I have read Beecher ('The measurement of pain', *Pharmacological Reviews*, 1957, 9, p. 59) and know that these opium-derived analgesics exert their principal effect not on the original pain but on the psychological processing of that pain. At first the effect was to allay fear and induce calm, even ecstasy. But my increasing tolerance to large doses and my increasing need for the drug have led them to consider Pennybacker's idea ('Management of intractable pain', *Proceedings of the Royal Society of Medicine*, 1963, 56, p. 191) of leucotomy, meddling with the thalamus or with the frontal lobe.

* * *

Now I envisage the lachrymose mourning of my wife who loved me, there is the clearing of drawers, folding of vacated clothes.

'Here is the T-shirt and here are the denims he wore in the summer, well, he was then, and robust. Here is the green and red shirt

worn, I remember, as we walked together last year on his birthday. Here are the shoes he last wore – still in the treads of one heel

dry worms of mud and dead bracken remain from that day on Long
    Synalds.'
Empty, amorphous and cold, blue tubes of Levi's. She weeps.

* * *

'They feel worthlessness and emptiness without the deceased. "Now I am nothing." "Feel empty inside." (Loss of self-esteem.) They wish to believe the deceased is not dead. Happy and sad memories of the deceased. Concern for the deceased's missing life-enjoyment. "I am here not deserving to be alive while he is dead, unable to enjoy this lovely day." (Guilt.) "It is a dream; he'll be back tomorrow." (Need to deny the loss.) "I've disposed of his clothing." (Demonstrates *either* ability to relinquish bond to the deceased *or* compulsion to rid themselves of the pain which that clothing evokes.)'

* * *

Here are some of the things you'll need if it takes place at home: bed-care utensil set (inc. denture cup, kidney basin, bed pan &c.), large sheet of plastic, rented wheelchair, box of flexible drinking-straws, one bag disposable bed pads (the incontinent will use considerably more), large size disposable diapers (several boxes), thermometer, one bottle ethyl alcohol, cotton balls, lubricant, commode, a great many spare under-sheets, six washcloths.

Each nostril must be cleaned with a twist of tissue or cotton wool. Eyelids should be swabbed with wool swabs and warm normal saline, especially in the morning.

* * *

Since I deal daily with the incurable
I am familiar with a number of
similar cases – irrespective of
their social background, their reaction to
terminal pain democratises them.
Today I sat beside a dying Cockney
(detect a patronising tone? – OK,
the living *ought* to patronise the dying):

> 'The wife was upset, as she's never seen
> me like this. So I said "We've all of us
> got to go, Girl, I've ad a decent life;
> it's im in the next bed as I feels sad for,
> e's only young – they ad to stop is pain
> by a-leucotomising-of is brain." '

* * *

[He writes] *Dear* [names of the Managing Director and one of the editors of his publishers], *I am irritated to learn that I shall soon be dead. You will be irritated to learn that by then I shall have completed a final book. This epistle constitutes one of its 100 sections. I shall be dead by the time you receive this typescript. Set it in the old way – in Tedious Acrimonious roman and Poppa-Piccolino italic on hand-deckled ipecacuanha leaf bound in reversed brushed papoose.* [He signs his name.]

PS. Seriously, though, my wife will deal with proof correction.

* * *

[*Ubi sunt* the beldam who collapsed in PRIDE OF PLAICE, the micro-palaeontologist with C. ventriculi, the hag carried off by ambulance from Azalea Terrace, the loon barbiturate ingester, the Master of the 100 100-Word Units, the C3 sniper victim, the lady with C. uterine cervix, the lady with breast cancer, the gent with bladder ditto, Epicurus, the jet-set exec-looking Head of Fine Art (snuff sternutator), the leucotomised folk-singer (singin whack for my diddle), &c.? All planted, at the time of going to press. Some feared oblivion; most feared pain. Poor frail dear frightened little vulnerable creatures.]

* * *

so long as we exist death
is not with us;
but when death comes,
then we do not exist.
The diseases of my
bladder
and stomach are pursuing [Pah.]
their course, lacking
nothing of their usual
severity; but against all
this is the joy in
my heart at the

I knew what I'd got, I'd
seen it in my notes,
looked it up in the
medical books, knew I
couldn't recover.
Wanted
to talk about it with
the doc but he always
seemed too busy, or just
called it inflammation
Oh love, don't go, stay;
hold my hand, *tight*, love

* * *

I have administered anti-emetics and stool softeners and allowed him to eat and drink. He seems free of pain and nausea but vomits periodically whilst remaining comfortable. He describes the sensation as being similar to defecating – relieving an uncomfortable fullness. I treat his ascites with the insertion of a LeVeen shunt. Unfortunately he has developed fungating growths and draining fistulae. Particularly troublesome are the fistulae in the perianal area originating from the urinary and intestinal tracts. I performed Turnbull's Diverting Loop Transverse Colostomy (see *Current Surgical Techniques*, Schering, 1978). Bloody oozing, odour and haemorrhage occur from his decubitus ulcers.

* * *

My fistulae ooze blood-and stink,
I vomit puce spawn in the sink,
diarrhoea is exuded.
Do not be deluded:
mortality's worse than you think.

You find the Limerick inapposite? Try the pretty Choriamb?

Bed-sores without; swarm-cells within.
Rancified puke speckles my sheets.
Faeces spurt out quite uncontrolled
into my bed, foetid and warm.
Vomit of blood tasting of brass,
streaked with green veins, splatters my face.

In vomiting, the glottis closes, the soft palate rises and the abdominal
muscles contract, expelling the stomach contents. In nausea, the
stomach relaxes and there is reverse peristalsis in the duodenum.

* * *

The list goes on and on interminably...
Rectal Bleeding, Chemotherapy
('Oh, how I dread the fortnightly injection –
the pain of it *itself*, and after that
ill for a week from the after-effects.
Anger is what I feel at dying, *anger* –
why can't the dropouts and the drunks get This?
I've always led such a clean, simple life...'),
Mastectomy, Metastases, Dyspnoea...
the list goes on and on and on and on...
(Some die in agony of mind and body
described by Hospice staff 'Dehumanised'.)
'Grief Work', 'Death Work', smug 'Terminal Caregivers'...
      I close my eyes but weep under the lids.

* * *

312

Crystalline water I sipped a few moments ago is returned as
vomit of discoloured filth, swarmjuice of rank-cancered gut.

C is for cardiac illnesses also – nothing to envy:
someone in High Street drops dead, shoppers, embarrassed/
       thrilled, gawp.

I can now vomit with accuracy and certain discretion
into the steel kidney-bowl, hourly they clear the puked slime.

Someone nocturnally, in the adjacent corridor, expires:
I hear a bloody great thud, then someone mutters 'Now, *lift*'.

I can no longer depend on my body doing my bidding:
ill bodies baulk at deep thoughts (of suicide and twee verse).

* * *

It is not as one can imagine beforehand. Dysgneusia (an altered
sense of taste occasionally occurring in cases of advanced malig-
nancy) prevents my savouring the cigar-box-spiciness, deep, round
fruitiness of the brick-red luscious '61 *Cheval Blanc*, the fat, buttery,
cooked, caramel-sweet-nuttiness of the 1894 Bual.

'He is a patient with dysgneusia and severe dysphagia and a fairly
advanced tumour for whom adequate hydration and nutrition are
maintained by frequent small feedings of liquids. The insertion of
an intraluminal esophageal tube is considered helpful. The dysphagia
is due to an obstruction in the esophagus and hypopharynx.'

* * *

An absorbent pad placed under the corner of the mouth at night will prevent dribbling causing wetness and discomfort. Ice may help stimulate muscle movement. Pass an ice cube from the corner of his mouth towards the ear, then dry the skin. It may help to wipe an ice cube round his lips, then dry them. (One of them had some movement in the eyelids and was able to blink Morse messages.) Phrase questions to receive very simple answers, e.g.: 'There is jelly and ice cream or egg custard – would you like jelly and ice cream?' Pyjamas should be absorbent.

* * *

Never had a husband. No one to care when it happened except Jesus. Pain. Radiotherapy. Terrible terrible pain. No one to care. Energy gone. Tired. So weak. Hair falling out. *Actually falling out!* Bald. Quite bald. The Good Book. Had to give me a wig, National Health – couldn't've afforded it myself. Always put my trust in the Lord. Never missed a Sunday. But now, somehow…Oh what will happen? Oh Gentle Jesus meek and mild oh Gentle Jesus help me *save* me Gentle Jesus the Good Book, *Revelation*, vi. 8. Of course Mr Tucker comes to help, a real help.

* * *

In Ashes Valley this evening I crawl under
     sheltering bushes
Joined at the same stock, so close together they
     let no light through them
And where no rain can pelt through their meshed roof, so
     knitted together
One with the other they grow. And I merge myself
     into the brown husks.
Weakly I rake together a litter from
     dry leaves that lie here
Deeply sufficient to succour two or
     three if they wanted
Warmth against Winter however malicious the
     elements' onslaughts.
Thus do I bury me closely with leaf-mould and
     wait for Athene's
Soft anaesthetic, benign soporific, ar-
     cane analgesic...

* * *

...by a vagrant.
There was an empty
bottle, and, oddly,
a glass and decanter
– rather posh ones.
There was no money.
Oh, yes, and this
page of note-pad...

*final lines of the sestet
of the final Petrarchan.
'Hollow' forms the first
c. I require dcdee. 'Follow'
could be the second c.*

*No. Something more prosy
for this job. The morphine,
the colostomy – fuck-all
there to justify lyric/metre.
But some structure still?
Why? Dignity? – bollocks.*

*But some structure still,
incongruously...*

*... 100 units each of 100 words.
How about that? Neat. One unit
per day for 100 final days*

* * *

316

Precambrian sub-division *Longmyndian*, ca. 600 million yrs. old. An individual Holocene *H. sapiens* with terminal pathogen. The coincidence of these two, thus: approaching oblivion (by ingestion of soporifics), *H. sap.* picks up, from scree in Ashes Hollow, a sample of rock imprinted with 600-million-year-old rain-pits. Suddenly, alas, the subtle grafting of a cdcdee Spenserian sestet onto an abbaabba Petrarchan octave does not matter. Vita b.; ars b. Nor does the Precambrian sub-division *Longmyndian*, ca. 600 million yrs. old, nor Holocene *H. sap* with terminal &c., nor the *conception* of its not mattering, nor

* * *

(The suicide is untrue. Bodily weakness prevents my moving from the bed. The dismay to my wife and child which suicide would occasion renders such a course untenable. They would interpret my self-destruction as failure on their part to nurse me properly. Conversely, the grief my daily decline causes them is difficult for me to bear. If I could only end the terrible work and unpleasantness I cause them... But bodily weakness prevents my moving from the bed. Shit gushes unbidden from the artificial anus on my abdomen. My wife patiently washes my faece-besmirched pyjamas, for *prosaic* love.)